DR. JACOB YOUMANS

MISSIONAL U

Life As a Mission Trip

TRI-PILLAR PUBLISHING

MISSIONAL U

Tri-Pillar Publishing
Anaheim Hills, California
Website: www.TriPillarPublishing.com
e-mail: tripillarpublishing@cox.net

International Standard Book Number --13:   978-0-9818923-6-8

International Standard Book Number --10:   0-9818923-6-1

Library of Congress Control Number: 2013939607

First edition, May, 2013

Printed in the United States of America

This book is dedicated to all of the people whom I have ever had the privilege of serving with on a mission trip. You all have taught me so much! Thanks for being an inspiration and for living out your faith! I wish I could list you all out by name – but that would take forever. You know who you are, and please know how much I appreciate you!

Contents

Contents *(continued)*

Contents *(continued)*

Acknowledgments

The following "thank-yous" are to people who have contributed to either *Missional U: Life As a Mission Trip* or *Missional Too: The Trip of a Lifetime*. This is our first time having "twins," so obviously there are many, many people to thank!

To Jesus, the Ultimate Teacher, who has pushed, prodded, molded, scolded, and refined me in ways that I am going to be processing for the rest of my life! Thank You for calling me to be on mission – and for surrounding me with an incredible community to be on mission with!

To the people of Our Savior Lutheran Church, Aiea, Hawaii; St. Paul's Lutheran Church, Orange, CA; and Concordia University Texas for allowing me to be on mission with you! You have all been so gracious in listening to these stories over and over again. Thanks for living them with me!

To all of the personal mission perspective writers: Thanks for your love and support! Specifically…

- To Matt Wingert: As I have been telling you for years, I'm excited to see what God's going to do with you! Never lose your passion for missions. You are most alive when you are on mission!

- To Cary Hoff: As of this publishing, you should be off to your next adventure in Vietnam. Now I've got to plan a mission trip out there! Proud of you!

- To Paul Stark: For the past decade you have watched the development of these books. Sometimes alongside, sometimes in prayers from afar – but always with excitement and passion! Thanks for always pushing and encouraging me to keep going – even when I feel like quitting!

- To Amanda White: As of this publishing, your next "around the world adventure" will be your greatest! Eleven countries in twelve months! Blessings on your travels!

- To Dave Talmage: You have been with me on more trips than I can count! You have been with me to more countries than anyone else! Thanks for always believing in a different way to do youth ministry!

- To Nick Miner: Your name may be "miner," but you were my rock during my St. Paul's years. Thanks for always being up for the adventure – and viewing life as one big game of "Risk!"

- To Ken Chitwood: I am so glad that God keeps bringing you back into my life! Thanks for helping to teach my Missional Leadership class at Concordia, and for always thinking differently!

- To Emily Eltiste: Now that you're a real live DCE, I'm excited to hear about all of your mission stories with your youth ministry! I'm excited to watch you raise up more missionaries!

- To Andrea Bolognini, the Concordia Texas legend – the first CTX DCE to do an international internship: Look at what you started! Thanks for believing in the "new guy!"

- To Nicole Seals: When I think about how far you have come in the last few years, I get goose bumps! From first-time mission trip participant to full-time missionary is unheard of! I'm excited to watch God use you in Australia!

- To Maile and Leilani Youmans: Your writing is getting so good! I cannot wait until you write *Missional U for Kids*! I hope you are as proud of your work as I am of you!

- To Lydia Humphries: You have been the answer to a decade-long prayer! Thank you for loving and serving alongside the Apache people! There are so many people that thank God for you being called there!

To Pastor Reno and the Apache people: I have spent more nights asleep on the Rez than anywhere outside of my own home. Thank you for allowing me into the Apache family! You have already taught me enough to process for the rest of my life, and I know we're not done yet!

To Ben Waldron and Daniel Wheel, for letting me crash your personal lake house retreat where I started writing this series! Thanks guys for your love and support!

To Paul Stark: I am so honored that you would write the foreword to *Missional U*. You are awesome! And you telling me that "reading this book is like sitting by the firepit back home" is one of the greatest compliments! It's been too long since we had a good firepit time. I guess I really only have one question for you: When are we going to work together again?!

To Ken Chitwood: Your foreword for *Missional Too* is absolutely fantastic! I am so thankful for your partnership in ministry! My students lovingly call you "the Lutheran Rob Bell," and I hope you see the huge compliment in there! You have an incredibly natural ability to make the simple profound, and the profound simple. I am curious and excited to see what God has lined up for you next!

To Peter Dibble: Thanks for another creative and eye-catching design! You make me look so much better than I deserve.

To Josephine and Andy Dibble and the Tri-Pillar family: I do not know how you do it all! You take my simple ideas and stories and painstakingly polish them up so they come out shining like the sun! And the best part is, the shining is a reflection of God's Son – Jesus – the Lord and Savior of the world! Thank you so much for believing in the *Missional U* series, and making this happen!

To my parents, Kim and Sandra Youmans, who from the beginning opened our home to be a mission outpost: Everyone was welcome. No one was ever turned away! Thanks for modeling all of this to me!

To Maile and Leilani: It is not a coincidence that in the process of writing of these books, you got to go on your first mission trip. I am amazed at how God uses you as missionaries now at ages 8 and 9, and I cannot wait to see what dreams He has for you as you grow! I love how seriously you take the call to be missional at your school and in the neighborhood. Jesus' love shines through you in all that you do. And I am so honored that I get to have you call me "Daddy!" I love you girls!

To my amazing wife Christy: When I first asked you out you said, "No, I have to go to a Mission Club meeting." I am pretty sure you were just blowing me off – but it's funny how 19 years later we're now on mission together! Christy, you have taught me so much about what it means to be missional. Your family's coming to faith story, that I am now a part of, has changed my life forever. I love you and am so honored to be on mission with you for the rest of our lives! I know you hate the cold – but can we please go visit Antarctica?

To God – Father, Son, and Holy Spirit: We thank You for the gift of life, the gift of New Life, and the calling to be Your missionaries!

Foreword

I still remember the first in-depth conversation I ever had with Jacob Youmans about life and ministry. Brand-new colleagues and still getting to know each other, we were having breakfast one morning at Norm's, an iconic Southern California diner known for hot coffee and cheap food. We were discussing the haplessness of the Cleveland Browns when all at once, in the middle of his poached eggs and swirly rye toast, he looked up at me and asked, "So Pauly, what's your pastoral approach to mission?"

My pastoral approach to mission? What kind of a question was that? I didn't answer him at first, partly because I had no idea what he was talking about. I didn't have any kind of approach to mission at all, much less a pastoral one. Feeling hapless myself, I gamely attempted a response to his question, but by then it was already clear to both of us that I had been completely blindsided by the inquiry. In truth, the mission question was a troubling one that gave me pause. While I had been on several mission trips over the years, I had never considered their place in the larger context of my ministry.

There at the table, I began to pull up some memories: Faded pictures mounted on out-of-the-way bulletin boards in the corner of the church narthex. Slideshow presentations on out-of-the-way countries shown in Sunday School. Glossy newsletters in the family mailbox mixed in with the bills and the junk mail. Unfamiliar people in strange clothes mixed in with the regular parishioners at the church potluck on Mission Festival Sunday. Apart from saving soup can labels and canceled postage stamps to give to the women's auxiliary (the reason for which was never explained to me), this was the sum total of all I had known in my life with regard to missions, missionaries, or indeed, anything having to do with the *Missio Dei* at all. While I reflected on that rather startling realization, another thought crossed my mind. As a typical church person from a typical church family who attended a typical church, I probably wasn't alone in my experience. There must be, I surmised, a lot of people out there just like me. You may be one of them.

And it's true. Many of us have a similar story to tell. Growing up, the idea of missions was foreign to us – as foreign as the slideshow countries where all those strangely dressed missionaries served. The mission field was a faraway place where other people went to do the bidding of God. "Mission Work" was a warm, fuzzy concept we viewed rather nonchalantly at arm's length, and most of us were happy to keep it there, safely mounted on those bulletin boards in the narthex.

But as I talked with Jake, I began to recognize something. There's a problem with that mind-set. It's skewed. It's culturally conditioned rather than Scripturally informed. Worst of all, it contributes to what for many people has become a severely limiting, unbiblical stereotype of the Great Commission... one which assumes that the call to Go and Tell is only for certain people, and which by definition is a distant, faraway activity.

As I listened to my new friend share about his passion for the lost and his commitment to selfless service in the name of Christ, as I heard him enthusiastically frame the idea of mission as a lifestyle rather than an event, when I caught the fact that all he was describing was a verb instead of a noun, something in me started to awaken. Seeds of change began to sprout. In that restaurant over poached eggs and toast, I tasted something new – something that has ever since flavored the way I look at life, ministry, and the very purpose for which God created, redeemed, and sustains me as His child.

When those of us in Christian circles think of the word "mission," we almost always connect it to the word "trip," or "field," or to the classical and Medieval Latin suffix "-ary" to denote the kind of person who takes said trips into said fields. That's all well and good as far as it goes. But with the book you are holding, Jacob Youmans's goal is to take you the rest of the way there – to help you understand mission in its fullest sense as a life-encompassing journey rather than a short-term service project or a career that people other than yourself have chosen as their life's work.

To be sure, to go on a mission trip is to share in a wonderful participatory event. It's something everyone should be encouraged to experience, and experience often. Mission trips are by definition couched in excitement and adventure. They have a certain exoticism about them. They hold opportunities for deep spiritual growth, memory-making, friendship-building, and a host of other intangibles that make them appealing to consider. Get outside your home state, or better yet your home country, and the prospect becomes still more exciting. Unknowns increase exponentially in a foreign setting, and that in turn kicks everything up a notch on the Official Mission Trip Anticipation Scale. Most important, of course, is the serving and sharing element inherent in a mission trip. It's the reason most of us go in the first place. We want to get out of our comfort zone and roll up our sleeves to serve the Lord. We want to feel good knowing that at the end of the day our efforts have contributed to needs being met, hope being reborn, and Jesus being shared – sometimes without any words being spoken at all.

But here's the great, grand question of the day: *What happens when we get home?* Does the work stop once the trip has ended? Do we disengage from a missional mind-set when we return to our own turf? Do we just wait around until the next opportunity comes before we mobilize again? Dr. Youmans – and far more significantly, the Scriptures –give an emphatic *No* to these questions, and in essence, that's why this book has been written. It is to help us revel in the joyful, earthy simplicity of a life continually positioned to do the Lord's bidding, and to give us a vision to see the pining need people have for Christ – not just in South America, but in South Bend, Indiana and South Haven, Michigan and South Central Los Angeles. When we spend our hard-earned cash to go and tell about Jesus in the hinterlands for a few days each year, we know we've made an investment in things of eternal consequence. But *Missional U* reminds us that it is of no less value and consequence when we make those investments in the lives of folks in our own community.

Why? It's because the Great Commission is a calling that encompasses everyone in every place. It's as close to us as our front porch or our back deck, and sometimes even closer than that. Our Lord's call to go and make disciples isn't confined to the act of going on a mission trip; it's about living a missional life. And the beautiful thing about this book is that in it you will receive a generous taste of what that life genuinely looks like... a taste that is sure to flavor your own life and sense of missional identity as a follower of Christ.

If you're like me, then you recognize what an incredibly exciting invitation lies just ahead. But you might also recognize a bit of hesitancy within yourself as you wonder how in the world your life could ever undergo such a radical shift. If so, then I have one more bit of good news for you. Jacob Youmans cannot blink without seeing the Great

Commission implications present in any given set of circumstances. He thrives on taking ordinary situations and transforming them into extraordinary opportunities for the Kingdom of God. He looks at the world through redemptive eyes, and he knows that in the course of a typical day there will always be openings for him to speak the truth of Jesus into someone's life. Here is a man who looks into our messy, chaotic, noisy world and sees the beauty of a hope-wielding, life-restoring, sin-forgiving Savior in the midst of it all. His life's mission is that this beauty would elude no one. He wants to share that mission with his friends, and he considers you his friend! In the pages ahead, be assured that he will show you, by personal example, how to make that shift a reality.

You have a marvelous, entertaining, emotionally compelling read in front of you. Immerse yourself in the missional world that's about to be presented. Feel the love on each page. Invest in the moment. You will come away powerfully changed.

Rev. Paul Stark
Webster County, Missouri

Introduction

What is Missional?

Welcome to Missional University! Let's start your training with the word "missional." The first time I heard this word, I lovingly yelled at my good friend Paul Stark for using it, informing him that he cannot just make up words. But now the word is everywhere. Here, in writing, I acknowledge that Paul was right and I was wrong!

I don't know if I have ever seen a bigger ministry buzz word than missional. As I meet people in ministry around the world, it's the word on the tip of everyone's tongue. But as I get into conversations, I hear many different definitions, ideas, philosophies, and lived-out practices. What does missional really mean?

Wikipedia® quotes the Oxford dictionary and says that missional means "relating to or connected with a religious *mission.*" Now, I do not want to offend Oxford – and more importantly, Wikipedia – but I think missional is so much bigger than that. It's not a program or an event. It's a lifestyle – a way of life that seeks purpose and meaning in what others see as randomness and coincidence. And here is the Missional U working definition: *Missional means living life as a mission trip.* Every moment of our lives could be a moment to share the Gospel in our words and actions. Every moment. There is no coincidence. There is no accident. There is no off switch to it. Every moment can be a moment to share the Gospel.

Let me describe for you my Missional U training. I'm what some people have affectionately called a "mission trip junkie." I get energized from a mission trip like nothing else. When I'm on a mission trip, I'm already planning how I can get back there.

I have led teams with junior high and high school students, college students, and adults. I've served alongside a truly wide variety of people and personalities. The oldest person I ever led on the mission field was a woman in her late 80s – and she carted bricks in a wheelbarrow all day long! And the youngest person was my two-year-old daughter who served with us at the Ronald McDonald House in Orange County, California. They had a policy that volunteers need to be at least two years old… Otherwise I would have brought her sooner! There are no age restrictions or limitations at Missional U!

By the grace of God, I have had the privilege of serving on short-term mission teams on every continent – except for Antarctica. (But people don't really live there, so I don't know if I'm ever going to get there!) My Missional U training ground has been the world. Please know that I'm not telling you this to boast in any way. That's not at all where my heart is. I never planned to travel so much that I'd get to every inhabited continent. It just happened. God opened doors, and I walked through them. Traveling extensively has enabled me to work in numerous multicultural settings, and with so many different missionaries. These experiences have taught me things I could not have learned any other way. In the mission field, like in the classroom, I tend to learn things the hard way. But I have learned an incredible amount during my travels!

Christy, my beautiful, wonderful, amazing wife, was born in Taiwan and her mother came to faith in Jesus through a Chinese missionary in Hawaii. My relationship with Christy is a large part of why I think so missionally! I'm just a lifelong, nerdy Lutheran boy. But I married into a family where missionaries have been used by God with miraculous results! Christy and I have been saying our next call will be overseas. Actually, we've been saying that since waiting for our very first call... However, God has not yet opened that door, at least not for a long-term call.

I find interacting with missionaries to be fascinating! They are all very different and yet have many similarities. I could focus on their differences all day long, but the biggest similarity I've seen in both short-term and long-term missionaries is they are very intentional about everything. They view every moment of the experience as an opportunity to communicate the Gospel. No movement is wasted. They live out the song, "Every move I make, I make in You!"[1] And everything is lifted up and surrounded in prayer – prayer support that is local and global, intentional and crucial. I haven't met a missionary yet who has underemphasized prayer. They also live in God's Word. The Scriptures are treasured and used not just as a textbook but as a guidebook.

Why can't everyday life be like that? I was tempted to begin this book with statistics on the state of Christianity in America. It's sad – no doubt about it. But others can give those statistics to you, and my guess is if you're reading this book you know that the situation is serious. You know that everyday life *needs* to be like a mission trip. You've enrolled in Missional U, after all! You know that the moment you leave your house, you are entering the mission field. In fact, many of you have a mission field right in your own home!

So this is what this book explores: *What would it be like if we lived life as a mission trip?* Is it even possible? Is it sustainable? What would it look like? Wasn't this Jesus' design for His followers and the Church all along? This book is your Missional University text book. We will go through stories I've accumulated from my "classroom of life," and you will be challenged to live out these lessons in your own classroom. The title of this book is also a play on words, where the dream and the goal is that by God's grace you will become a more missional "you." Like most good college courses, this will not be easy – especially if you take it seriously. But with a little patience and practice, you will be amazed at what God will do in you and through you!

Can I Get a Witness?!

To start, I want to draw your attention to Acts chapter 1. This is where St. Luke describes for us again (the first time is Luke 24:50-52) the Ascension account. Just before Jesus is taken up into heaven, He says in Acts 1:8, **"you will be my witnesses in Jerusalem, and in all Judea and Samaria, and to the ends of the earth."** As with all of Jesus' words, I believe He chose those words – and in this case those geographical locations – very specifically.

Before we get into geography, though, let's focus on the word "witness." Jesus tells us that we will be His witnesses. Eyewitnesses today are not always known for their reliability in court, but in an ancient Jewish court of law they were very significant. They were crucial to the entire case. In fact, there was no case without them!

Deuteronomy 19:15, written ~ 1,500 years before Jesus but still followed strictly in Jesus' time, says: **"One witness is not enough to convict anyone accused of any crime or offense they may have committed. A matter must be established by the testimony of two or three witnesses."** Witnesses were crucial. Witnesses were the proof required to convict someone. And one witness was not enough... There needed to be two or three! So when Jesus says we are His witnesses, He is saying we are His proof! Together, we are the proof that He exists, that He loves, that He saves, that He lives, and that He's coming to take us home. Establishing proof for something is a major responsibility!

Let's view Matthew 16:13-17 through the lens of witnesses:

> **He (Jesus) asked his disciples, "Who do people say the Son of Man is?"**
>
> **They replied, "Some say John the Baptist; others say Elijah; and still others, Jeremiah or one of the prophets."**
>
> **"But what about you?" he asked. "Who do you say I am?"**
>
> **Simon Peter answered, "You are the Messiah, the Son of the living God."**
>
> **Jesus replied, "Blessed are you, Simon son of Jonah, for this was not revealed to you by flesh and blood, but by my Father in heaven."**

Jesus is preparing them to be eyewitnesses! He's showing them what it means to be "proof." He's teaching them to avoid the distractions and lies of the world, and to focus on the truth. I believe the question, *Who do you say Jesus is?* is at the heart of being missional. If you haven't wrestled with this question before – today's the day! Our words, and perhaps more importantly our lives and how we travel through the trials and realities of life, all communicate that Jesus is the Messiah – the Savior of the world! Being a living-proof witness is a huge responsibility, but it also leads to incredible opportunities to help people know the truth!

Geography 101

Now, for the specific geographical locations, Jesus says **"Jerusalem, and in all Judea and Samaria, and to the ends of the earth."** Some have argued that Jesus wants this to be a "progression," like a ladder where you just keep going up and up until you reach the top. But Jesus does not say Jerusalem, *then* Judea, *then* Samaria, and *then* the ends of the earth. Others have argued that this is a list of "options," like a multiple choice quiz where one simply needs to pick an answer and stick with it. But Jesus does not say Jerusalem, *or* Judea, *or* Samaria, *or* the ends of the earth.

I would argue that **"Jerusalem, and in all Judea and Samaria, and to the ends of the earth"** is all-inclusive. It *has* to be all-inclusive. We're called to be witnesses – "proof" – in Jerusalem, *and* in Judea, *and* in Samaria, *and* to the ends of the earth. *Everywhere!* That's the missional life! It's viewing the entire world – home, near, far, and everywhere – as the mission field. It is seeing every human encounter and relationship as an opportunity to share the Gospel!

Some have argued that Jerusalem, Judea, Samaria, and the ends of the earth are convertible to city, state, country, and world in today's context. But as we look closely at these specific geographical locations, some additional concepts arise.

Jerusalem

Jerusalem is the holy city (Isaiah 52:1). At the time of Jesus' ministry, it's where the "in crowd" – the "Jew's Jew" – lived. In the Old Testament book of Nehemiah, we are reminded of the importance of the holy city. Nehemiah led the charge to rebuild the walls around the city to protect those inside and keep out those who meant to do harm. It was a safe place – a sanctuary from the cruelty of the outside world. I like to view my "Jerusalem" as my church, and, in a broader sense, all the people of God – Christians around the world who know Jesus as their Lord and Savior. We can be missional with Christians too!

To be complete, I view metaphorical Jerusalem as also including visitors who come to be with us for worship, Bible study, or similar spiritual activity, even if they are still unbelievers at this point, provided they are coming because of a sincere interest. After all – they have come to the holy city, as it were, and that is Jerusalem!

Speaking of visiting churches, I have the privilege of visiting a wide variety of churches in my current role at Concordia University Texas. Many of the churches I visit have a sign at the parking lot exit that reads: "You are Now Entering the Mission Field." Maybe your church has this sign. But there was one church I visited that had this message on *both* sides of the sign pole! So as people drove into the church parking lot, they were reminded that the church building and property are a mission field as well! So the question is: *How can I be a witness to fellow Christians and others who have a sincere interest in Christianity?*

Judea

Judea was a much larger area geographically, within which was located the city of Jerusalem. While inhabitants of Judea were mainly Jews, they generally did not have the same status as inhabitants of Jerusalem.

Metaphorically speaking, I view our "Judea" as people who are not Christian but are otherwise similar to us. Maybe they have the same socioeconomic status. Maybe they have similar ethnic or cultural backgrounds. These are people who are generally disinterested and possibly even a bit uncomfortable walking into our church, having relatively little interest in spiritual matters. *How can I be a witness to people who are like me except generally disinterested in Christianity?*

Samaria

Samaria is the name given to the Northern Kingdom, which was entirely separated from the city of Jerusalem. In Jesus' time, Samaritans were viewed very harshly by the Jewish people. They were not "pure Jews," being essentially half Jew and half Assyrian. Their hybrid status caused them to be viewed by many as even lower than the Gentiles. Samaritans were hated and despised by the Jews, which made Jesus' encounter with a Samaritan woman in John chapter 4 so powerful, and similarly His parable of the Good Samaritan (Luke 10).

We can view our "Samaria" as people who are in many ways *not* like us. Maybe they have significantly less or more financial means than we do. Maybe they have a different skin color. Maybe they speak a different language. Odds are, if they walked into our church, they would not feel comfortable at first. *How can I be a witness to people who are not like me?*

Ends of the Earth

You might think "Ends of the Earth" is rather self-explanatory, but let me explain it anyway. By now, you can see that I'm treating the regions metaphorically. So, continuing in this way, I define Ends of the Earth as people who have literally almost nothing in common with me, aside from our humanity. We share very few similarities when it comes to things like race, ancestry, culture, historical/ political/economic context. These people might live right next door to us, although if so, they may be relative newcomers to our country who haven't had much time to assimilate. They may speak English, although it probably isn't their first language and there's a good chance they aren't fluent.

Whether we meet them on our evening walk in our neighborhood or on a business trip to a country we've never been to before, it really doesn't matter – because all over this planet, this third rock from the sun, there are human beings who need a witness who can "speak their language" (not necessarily with spoken words), love them for who they are, and share the grace, mercy, and love we have in Jesus! The Ends of the Earth could be at the end of your street, or it could be halfway around the world, but the call is to be His witnesses to these people. *How can I be a witness to the Ends of the Earth?*

. . . . .

All of the stories from the mission field will be divided into these four sections: Jerusalem, Judea, Samaria, and the Ends of the Earth. While I'm normally not a fan of "compartments," I'm doing this to show you the wide variety of mission and ministry opportunities that are around us every day. My hope and prayer is that they will inspire you to look at your world differently, and seek ways to be a witness as you live your life as a mission trip – wherever God leads you!

Traveling from the Ends of the Earth to Jerusalem

Now that I've given you the basics of how I view the four regions, let's talk about them all together. I've already given some insight into how people in the different regions relate to us on mainly a secular level: cultural differences, socio-economic differences, personality differences, etc. Let's get a little deeper into spiritual differences. Here's how I see the four regions from the perspective of religious context:

- The inhabitants of Jerusalem (don't forget, I'm speaking metaphorically) are Christians or are showing a true interest in becoming a Christian.
- The inhabitants of Judea are respectful of Christianity, and probably even consider it their "default religion," and yet they have no real interest in worship or living a Christian life. Many so-called "Christmas/Easter Christians" are actually residing in Judea. To be sure, most citizens of the U.S. – a "Christian country" – spend their life not traveling outside of Judea.

- The inhabitants of Samaria are generally opposed to Christianity. They may have a "default religion" of their own – but this time it's non-Christian. Or perhaps they are simply apathetic when it comes to spirituality, even to the extent of referring to themselves as atheist if backed into a corner.
- Those who live at the Ends of the Earth are generally more strongly opposed to Christianity, often being a devote follower of another religion or strongly atheist.

To live a missional life, by the power of God we continually look for ways to guide others from wherever they are outside of Jerusalem into the holy city. And this should not be an occasional pilgrimage... The goal is for them to pull up stakes and make Jerusalem their permanent home.

In the ancient world, things were more compartmentalized geographically. Differences such as those I've touched on were more commonly accompanied by geographical differences as well. However, today's world is so much more interconnected. This provides us with opportunities the early Church simply didn't have. People from vastly different cultures and religious backgrounds than ours now routinely move into our neighborhoods, attend our schools, play on our soccer teams, carpool with us to work – you name it. Today, I can walk down my street, right here in our "Christian country," and be missional at the Ends of the Earth. And tomorrow I can hop on a plane and travel halfway across the world, to a "non-Christian country," and be missional in Jerusalem.

Like most people, I love to travel – except for one thing... It takes such a long time to get from here to there! *"Beam me up, Scotty!"* works on TV, but not in this galaxy. (Believe me, I've tried!) Being patient on a long journey can be tough.

In a similar way, when we are acting as guides (and we ourselves are following Jesus) to folks who are taking their metaphorical journey from wherever they started to Jerusalem, we need to patient. After all, the Ends of the Earth is a long, long way from the holy city. Usually there are stops along the way in Samaria, but hopefully we can make it to Judea before nightfall. Once our companion makes it to Judea, that's when friendships can form and trust can be built. Come morning, the walls of the holy city just might be visible on the horizon, and feeling refreshed we can make it there soon. (Are you with me?)

Extra Credit

Interspersed through the *Missional U* stories, you will find selections from my "top ten" list that I have gone over with participants on just about every mission trip I've ever led. I call it *The Top Ten Ways to Ruin a Mission Trip*. This list has been created over many years of participating in mission trips and watching missionaries wrestle with these issues. This is a list of surefire ways to derail any mission trip!

But as you read the list of mission trip no-nos, be reminded that God's grace is bigger. Even in our sin and screw-ups, God still works! We humbly cling to the promise of Romans 8:28, **"that in all things God works for the good of those who love him, who have been called according to his purpose."** Even when we make mistakes, God still somehow works it for good in His miraculous way. While this list is designed to inform you of some of the potential dangers and distractions, we trust that God's Word will not return void (cf. Isaiah 55:11). God is still God, and He will still work in us and through us!

In the second book of the *Missional U* series, *Missional Too*, another top ten list is given: *Top Ten Excuses for Why I Can't Go on a Mission Trip*. In those sections, we explore ten of my "favorite" excuses I've heard from potential missionaries. You or someone you know may be living in one of these excuses, and I hope I can show you ways to overcome any excuse and follow our God-given command to "go!" (cf. Matthew 28:19). Some of these excuses may sting a little as they hit a little too close to home. But hopefully you'll see how God can transform your reason not to go into an inspiration for yourself and others. People in the Old and New Testaments made excuses constantly – in fact, they used some of these very same excuses – and God still used them in miraculous ways! Even if you have an excuse or two, be prepared for God to work in you and through you such that, before you know it, you will GO!

I am also very thankful for twelve of God's servants, each of whom is living an exemplary missional life. Each has been kind enough to provide a personal mission perspective (six in *Missional U* and six in *Missional Too*). I have had the honor and privilege of serving with all them on various mission adventures, and I am so thankful for their partnership and wisdom. I know their insights will be a blessing to you as you train for your missional life. They have trained in their own Missional University for years, and I'm excited for them to be a part of this course.

Geography 201

But before we get into the stories from the mission field, I need to bring up two more geographical locations mentioned in Acts chapter 1. Picture it. The disciples are witnessing the Ascension of Jesus into heaven. They are looking at Him rise into the sky with, I'm assuming, their chins on the ground. They are wondering what's going on and what will be happening next, when all of a sudden **"two men dressed in white"** (verse 10) appear. It's safe to assume these are angels, even though we are never told specifically. And then they speak… **"'Men of Galilee,' they said, 'why do you stand here looking into the sky? This same Jesus, who has been taken from you into heaven, will come back in the same way you have seen him go into heaven.'"** (verse 11) Angels always say the darndest things!

Did you catch the other two geographical locations? **"Men of Galilee,"** the angels say. Galilee is their home. It's where they are from. I'm sure they have lots of family and friends back in Galilee. But I find it fascinating that they are reminded of their hometown right after they are told to be witnesses in Jerusalem, and in Judea, and in Samaria, and to the ends of the earth. Is this really a time to be bringing up home?

Maybe the angels are reminding them that everything has changed. What they have thought of as home is no longer their home. Their home is now Jerusalem, Judea, Samaria, and the ends of the earth. Being a witness, being proof, being on a mission trip, is too big a calling for someone just to remain in Galilee. The whole world needs to hear their testimony. For us too – we cannot stay at "home." We need to go. For Jesus, we need to willingly leave the comforts and confines of "home" to be His witnesses throughout the world.

The second geographical place? You may not have caught this one… Heaven! Heaven is geography. And for witnesses of Jesus – for all who believe in Him as Lord and Savior – heaven is our *new* home! By God's power and guidance, being missional is about helping as many people as possible claim heaven as their home. Being missional is about a fuller heaven. Being missional is about a mission trip where heaven is the destination. May it be so!

Dr. Jacob Youmans
Austin, Texas
May, 2013

Jerusalem

Introduction to Jerusalem

There may not be a more important city in the history of the world than Jerusalem. Geographically, Jerusalem is the ancient capital of Israel. It's the heart of the Promised Land that Moses only saw from afar (Deuteronomy 34:1-4). It's the city of King David. It's where Solomon built the first temple. It's the place where Jesus had His triumphant entry on Palm Sunday… and on a hill in the outskirts He was killed on Good Friday. It's an ancient city and a holy city to Judaism, Christianity, and Islam. The meaning of the name Jerusalem in disputed. Some argue it means "foundation," while others insist that it means "holy" or "sanctuary."

These definitions tie nicely into the metaphorical meaning that we will be exploring as well. Jerusalem is your church. Jerusalem is the fellowship of believers around the world. It's the "inreach" to the outreach we hear so much about. Metaphorical Jerusalem is big. If you want to know how big, check out the counter at: http://dom.imb.org/the%20 unfinished%20task.htm.

The call to be a witness in Jerusalem brings you to the challenge of "witnessing to the witnesses." It's the challenge of sharing your faith in Jesus in an encouraging and inspiring way with those who already know Jesus Christ as Lord and Savior. This is the foundation of the missional life. It's the call to witness to the holy people too. You do not have to go anywhere to be a missionary. You can be a missionary right on the church property! You can be a servant to fellow believers as much as to not-yet-believers.

As we go through these adventures in this section, I encourage you to constantly be asking yourself what *your* Jerusalem looks like.

On to Jerusalem…

The Cactus

In Canyon Day, Arizona, on the White Mountain Apache Reservation, there is a particular mountaintop that I have been taking our groups to for years. It's not the tallest mountain on the reservation, but it's *our* mountain, just the same. It is the closest mountain to the Canyon Day Lighthouse Family Bible Church, our "home base" when we visit the reservation. We have conquered this mountain many times. It's certainly a manageable hike. It provides quite a challenge for some, and for the more experienced and adventurous hikers there are rock faces that are fun to climb as well.

From the top of this mountain, you can see pretty much the entire village of Canyon Day. It's beautiful and peaceful up there. We have had many awesome prayer sessions at the top of that mountain. We erected a cross at the summit in 2001, our first time there, and that cross remains to this day. It's a very special spot. Hiking up and down is a team effort. It's a community-building exercise as well as physical exercise. We make sure that everyone makes it to the top – and everyone makes it back down! The destination is spectacular, but the journey is equally beautiful. There isn't really a path, per se. Without a clearly marked trail, we just find a way to get to the top. We know our destination. The journey itself is a bit different every time. But there is one thing that's guaranteed each time – this mountain always provides an adventure!

On one of our more memorable trips, we got to the summit with minimal difficulties. But for one of our students, going down was a whole different story! This particular student was watching his step very carefully. He slowly went down the mountain, step by step, all the while on the lookout for snakes, loose rocks, cacti, and other prickly and pointy desert mountain things. Then – all of a sudden – he lost his footing, and before he knew it, his legs were up in the air and he landed with a loud thud – right on top of a large cactus! His bottom just so happened to cushion his fall. In fact, he could not have sat on that cactus any more perfectly if he had tried!

For a teenage boy trying to look tough and conquer this mountain, I cannot think of a more embarrassing situation. As he started to get up, it was obvious that part of the cactus was coming with him. In fact, it was attached in a most painful place – painful to the body *and* his pride! He screamed out in pain, but wisely did not touch the cactus as it would have stuck to his hand as well. His screams certainly got the attention of everyone else in our group, and once we saw him, we all knew he was going to be hurting for quite a while.

But in the midst of this unfortunate mishap, I had the privilege of witnessing a completely new illustration of unconditional love. Without even being asked, one of the college students helped up this cactus-pierced high school student, and took him behind a few bushes. With painstaking patience, he pulled every last cactus needle out of his friend's backside. He did it without any complaining. He did it without being grossed out by the location of the needles, or by the blood they produced. He did it with his friend wincing and groaning with every pull. He knew it was painful, but he also knew that those needles had to come out. He just wanted to get his friend back on the journey, and he knew this was not possible until every last needle was out of him.

This "medical operation" took quite a while, and I'm sure it felt especially long for the inflicted patient. But after twenty minutes or so, and plenty of double- and triple-checking for more, all of the needles were finally out. This young man was still plenty sore – and would continue to be quite uncomfortable for several days – but he made it down the mountain with the rest of the team. And the whole way down the mountain, he was hiking with his new best friend and thanking him for loving him enough to take out all of those cactus spines.

· · · · ·

When Jesus tells us to love our neighbor as ourselves in the Gospels of Matthew, Mark, and Luke – a theme we also see in Old Testament accounts in Leviticus and Deuteronomy – He isn't just defining our "neighbor" as non-Christians. He's referring to all of our neighbors; to *all* people. Too often, we think of "missions" as only serving those who do not know Jesus. While that certainly is missional (and very important!) we cannot forget about the mission to our brothers and sisters in Christ – to Jerusalem. We are called to live life as a mission trip *for* believers, not just *with* them. Believers and unbelievers both need to be viewed as neighbors, and served as part of the mission field. Interestingly enough, the question of *Who is my neighbor?* is one that Jesus had to answer multiple times.

The story of the Good Samaritan is one of the most famous parables of Jesus. Even many non-Christians have heard of this story. Many states and countries even have a "Good Samaritan Law," which means you have a legal obligation to provide reasonable aid and assistance to someone who is injured or incapacitated. This means it is against the law *not* to help your neighbor! You can read the full Good Samaritan story in Luke 10:25-37. The parable was the answer Jesus gave in response to the question: **"And who is my neighbor?"** (verse 29). I think it's important to note who is *not* a "neighbor" to the man who was beaten and left for dead in the story. In verses 31 and 32 we are told that a priest and a Levite did not help the person in need. I'm assuming you know what a priest is, and a Levite was a member of the tribe of Levi – one of the original twelve tribes of Israel. Moses was a Levite, and according to Numbers 18:2-6, Levites were chosen as a tribe to serve as "priests to the priests," and to take care of the tabernacle and eventually the temple. Priests and Levites were important spiritual leaders regarded as good, holy, God-fearing people.

The truly shocking moments for me in the Good Samaritan parable are when these two "church workers" do not stop to help someone in need. You would think that church workers, of all people, would be willing to help! But these two were not. Maybe they feared touching a dead body, which could make a man "unclean" by the law. Maybe they just assumed that someone else would help him. But the account specifically tells us that both men saw the injured man, and yet both passed him by. These leaders of Israel would not help a fellow Israelite. That's as absurd as a follower of Jesus not helping another follower of Jesus! We need to think about what our mission is to our church family. We need to be missional *within* the church too!

Those who know Jesus as Lord and Savior are not immune to problems, and certainly need our help too! Jesus says in Matthew 5:45 – **"He (God) causes his sun to rise on the evil and the good, and sends rain on the righteous and the unrighteous."** Good people and evil people fall on cacti, and what they have in common is that they both need help. They both need someone to take out the needles! Can you imagine what it would be like to try to get all of those cactus spines out of a part of your body that you cannot completely see? You would need help. You would need the care and the willingness of someone who loves you with an unconditional love. We should remember to be missional within our very own congregation, ministry group, and even family. This is crucial to understanding mission in Jerusalem.

We are called to serve our brothers and sisters in Christ, and help them however we can – even if they have a cactus spine in their backside. To ignore it and expect them to continue on the journey with it stuck inside of them would be harmful and cruel! To help them with the needle is a beautiful image of unconditional love. It might get a little messy when you get that needle out, but it's the only way to finish the journey. And we all want to make it through the journey together!

Questions for Reflection and Discussion

1. Who is your neighbor? In what ways are you "neighborly?"

2. How can you be missional within your own church?

3. Who do you know who already knows Jesus, but could still use a friend on life's journey? How can you be their friend?

The Key

How many people can you squeeze into one elevator? During a mission trip to Alaska, my group learned the answer to this question the hard way, in what ended up being one of the more terrifying events of my ministry. I had brought 19 students and three adults on a trip to connect with a church and the community on the Kenai Peninsula. After one particularly long day, we met together for group processing and Bible study, and then around 11 P.M. the students headed up to bed, ready for a good night's rest. Exhausted and not wanting to wait, all 19 students decided to climb into the elevator at once. Now, I should explain that this particular elevator was not located in a luxury hotel. It was in a small, four-story motel in middle-of-nowhere, Alaska. It was the kind of elevator where one might feel comfortable with about five or six people inside – certainly not 19!

I was down the hall in a meeting with my adult leaders, processing the events of the day and preparing for the next, when suddenly we heard a loud, metallic BOOM – followed immediately by screams of terror. Those screams still resound in my head. They were more piercing than anything I had ever heard. I ran down the long hallway as the screams continued. I quickly learned that the commotion was coming from the elevator shaft. The elevator cable had broken, and every single student I had brought on the trip was stuck in an elevator in middle-of-nowhere, Alaska! By the mercy and grace of God, I have never lost a student on a mission trip, but at that moment I wondered if I had lost every single one!

This was one of the biggest moments of panic in my ministry. While I could certainly hear their loud screams, I couldn't really communicate with them. I had absolutely no idea how we were going to get them out, and what was even more terrifying was that neither did the panic-stricken night manager. He just kept saying over and over again: "This has never happened before!"

One of the hotel employees quickly called the local fire department, but then warned me that "local" was a relative term in middle-of-nowhere, Alaska. While we waited for them to arrive, I tried every *Die Hard* move I could think of to get into that elevator. I tried prying the doors open with a crowbar – nothing. I tried to access the elevator from the back, but that wasn't going to work either. I used every ounce of my strength and ingenuity, and yet those elevator doors wouldn't budge. I was helpless, unable to do anything to get my students out. Finally, after about 45 minutes of my feeble attempts to rescue them, the *real* rescuers arrived. The fire trucks pulled up outside with lights flashing and horns blaring. The firemen calmly walked through the motel and, without saying a word, walked right up to the elevator, stuck a little stick into a peephole-sized opening in one of the doors, and instantly the doors flew open.

The elevator had dropped several feet below the floor, and we helped the students out one by one. They were all perfectly fine, very relieved and grateful to be rescued! I was so thankful to have everyone out, safe and sound. For the rest of the trip, all 19 of those students took the stairs!

I marveled at how quickly the firemen were able to get those elevator doors open. I had tried everything I could think of, and yet all my own efforts had failed. But once the key was inserted, those doors popped right open with no effort at all.

Think of how much stress and panicking could be avoided if we all just had "the key!" Without it, we are trapped in fear and chaos. But with the key, everything's under control. As we walk through Jerusalem, Judea, Samaria, and the Ends of the Earth, there is one key to keep us grounded and connected. This key leads to a spiritual health that enables us to keep going and going.

. . . . .

Jesus talks about this key throughout His ministry. In fact, His whole ministry is about this key. But He's never more direct than in Revelation chapter 1, as He tells St. John: **"Do not be afraid. I am the First and the Last. I am the Living One; I was dead, and now look, I am alive for ever and ever! And I hold the keys of death and Hades."** (verses 17-18) Jesus Himself is the key! This is not just knowledge about Jesus. James reminds us: **"You believe that there is one God. Good! Even the demons believe that."** (James 2:19) This key is much more than head knowledge. It's *heart* knowledge. It's a personal relationship with Jesus! It's a faith relationship where we lay all of our sin and shame at His feet, and trust in His undeserved grace and mercy. It's a personal relationship where we find our hope only in Him.

I find it interesting that even here, Jesus starts off with **"Do not be afraid."** (Revelation 1:17) The resurrected Jesus opens with this statement at most of His appearances. John had previously seen Him after the resurrection, and yet apparently there was still the need for Jesus to tell him not to be afraid. Holy fear is good! As Martin Luther says in his explanation of the commandments, we should fear and love God (*Small Catechism*). While we are awestruck by a glimpse of the power and glory of God, it is our natural response to be fearful as we see our own frail human weakness and sinfulness in the light of God's perfection. But Jesus tells us to fear not – we are in a relationship with Him. Fear not, because He loves us so much!

Jesus also reminds us that He's the First and the Last. He always was, and He always will be (cf. Revelation 1:8). He's God, but He is also true man – which means His suffering and death were very real and very painful. In fact, the pain of His crucifixion was intensified by the weight of the whole world's sins that He bore on His back. A body that had never experienced sin *became* sin (2 Corinthians 5:21). But He did not stay dead. Being true God, He rose from the dead, conquering death once and for all (1 Corinthians 15:20-26)!

Jesus is eternal, and so is His love for you and for me. His love conquers sin, death, and the devil. His love saves. For all who believe in Him, He is the key to eternal life! This simple truth almost seems *too* easy at times. We may find ourselves thinking there must be more that we need to do. Just as I had tried everything to get into that elevator, we are prone to look for more challenging and complicated ways to open the door to everlasting life. Man-made religions are very good at this. If you just do the right things, say the right things, jump through this hoop or that hoop – then you can earn your salvation. Every other belief system in the world is about what *we* do. The fascinating thing about our key is that it is only about what *Jesus* has done for us. Jesus is the key.

This key is meant to be shared. It cannot be hidden or kept quiet. The key is for everyone – God wants all people to come to full knowledge of Him (cf. 1 Timothy 2:4)! The missional life is about showing others the key. First we show them how the key works by modeling it in our own life, and then we share how the key can work in their life as well. It's all about faith in Jesus. Without this, the door will never be open – no matter how hard we try (Revelation 3:7).

Questions for Reflection and Discussion

1. How do you handle moments of panic? Do you try to solve the crisis yourself? Do you call the experts? Do you stop and pray for God's help and wisdom?

2. Have you ever found yourself looking for more challenging and complicated "keys" than the one Jesus has already given us? Explain.

3. What has "The Key" unlocked in your life?

4. Do you know someone who's been searching after the wrong "key?" How can you share Jesus with them?

Digging Ditches

What's said in the ditch stays in the ditch. This has been a key philosophy in much of my mission work. I've actually practiced this philosophy more times than I can count. When I am on certain mission trips, specifically the ones that involve difficult manual labor done in hot and uncomfortable conditions with minimal modern tools, I always ask for the most difficult job on the work site. That simple request usually gets me either tossed into a ditch, or told where to go dig a ditch! It turns out most people do not enjoy digging ditches. While this may seem like common sense to you, it was something I had to learn the hard way – many, many times. Trying to convince people to help me in the ditch has been an interesting experience as well!

But what they soon realize – if they accept my invitation – is that digging a ditch is a bonding experience like no other. It's hard, dirty, sweaty, stinky (literally and figuratively) work. However, it provides the ditch-diggers the time and proximity to talk about anything and everything. And interestingly enough, the deeper the ditch, the deeper the conversation goes. On a trip to El Salvador with Habitat for Humanity, I got to spend several days in the ditch with one of my college students, Amanda. Now, I thought I knew Amanda pretty well before the ditch – but afterward I knew her better than I ever would have expected!

While I cannot share with you everything we talked about (*What's said in the ditch stays in the ditch!*) I can tell you we discussed our pasts, our futures, our hopes, our dreams, our failures, our successes, and our callings – just to name a few of the lighter topics of conversation. We both have referred back to this time on several occasions and we know that God gave us a precious gift that day in that ditch. When I returned to Concordia Texas the following week, I told all of my coworkers how I wished I could spend several days in the ditch with each one of our students! They laughed – but they also knew that I wasn't joking! It would be an incredible way to learn a lot more about them – such as their past experiences, how they are wired, and what they think about the bigger life questions.

On another occasion, I was digging a ditch in Brazil. The trip became a tricultural experience because in addition to our group from North America and the native Brazilians we were working with, there was a group from Oxford, England. They were all college students, and connected very well with our group of college and high school students. The one challenge I did not anticipate was when the English students made it clear from the beginning that they were in Brazil mostly for a cultural experience, not a missional one. They hadn't come to do hard manual labor and to serve Jesus. Thus, they left the more difficult jobs to my team. A few feelings were hurt, and it would have been easy for our group to grow resentful of the situation, but I kept reminding our team that God was going to work through this whole process. We should just focus on doing our work to the best of our ability and to the glory of God. And that's exactly what they did! That was the most exhausting trip I have ever done – but I was so proud of my team!

One of the older English students, Stewart, was working on a Ph.D. in microbiology while working at a firm in the UK that is one of the top cancer research facilities on the planet. He was very curious as to why I was spending so much time in the ditch. I lovingly told him, "What happens in the ditch stays in the ditch." This made him even more curious! And sure enough, on the last day of work for their group (they were leaving a few days early to explore other parts of Brazil) Stewart descended into the ditch with me.

I will never forget that time with Stewart. Stewart was a proud and vocal atheist, but he grew up Anglican. In fact, his father is a deacon in the Anglican Church. While we spent those hours laboring in the ditch together, I learned just how brilliant a man Stewart is. If his name is ever in the newspaper as the guy who cured cancer, I won't be surprised at all. We talked honestly and openly as we worked. We went around and around in the ditch about faith and science, proof and belief – all in a very respectful way. I told him my story, and he told me his. We developed a mutual appreciation for one another, even though it was obvious to both of us that we were not going to see eye to eye on many things. I wish I could tell you more about what happened in that ditch, but of course I can't. *What's said in the ditch stays in the ditch.*

After a very long day of manual labor and mental work in that ditch, I went to bed early while my team stayed up and enjoyed the last night with our friends from England. The next day, after we said good-bye to the English team, my group asked me what I talked about with Stewart in the ditch. I reminded them of the cardinal rule of ditch-digging – which they completely respected – but then they said something that kicked-up my theology of the ditch even further. They said that as they processed the day with Stewart, he had commented how much he enjoyed being in the ditch with me.

When they asked him why, he said, "There's no room for BS in the ditch."

I didn't get to see a conversion of Stewart. In fact, I have never heard from him since that day in the ditch. But I pray that somehow the conversations we had about Jesus, love, mercy, sin, grace, and redemption will sink in, because Stewart knows there is no room for "BS" in the ditch.

. . . . .

There is a ministry of excellence. When the followers of Jesus work hard, people will notice. And when people notice, we have the opportunity to give God all of the glory and honor and praise! Even the menial stuff in life, like digging ditches – which many people would blow off and not think of as an opportunity for excellence – can be a means of communicating our devotion to Jesus. In fact, sometimes that message gets across even more effectively, because it stands out in the midst of an unpleasant circumstance where people don't expect to find it.

St. Paul addresses this in the book of Colossians. He says: **"Whatever you do, work at it with all your heart, as working for the Lord, not for human masters, since you know that you will receive an inheritance from the Lord as a reward. It is the Lord Christ you are serving."** (Colossians 3:23-24) Interestingly enough, Paul is addressing slaves with this comment. And if those who have no earthly freedom can focus on the bigger picture of serving God with their work, how much more should we – as the people who have the greatest freedom in the history of the world!

When I get stressed-out and feel like breaking, and when I am tired beyond imagination and feel like I can't go on, the most helpful thing for me is to remember that *all* of this is for Jesus. All of my blood, sweat, and tears are for Him. And I pray that people will see the excellence in my work and ask me *why*. I pray that people will see how I handle stress and ask me *how*. I pray that people will see how I keep going even when I want to quit, and ask *what* keeps me going. These questions all have the same "Sunday School answer" – Jesus! I am striving to work for God, not for men. And in my service to men, I truly pray that God is glorified. I always try to remind myself – and others – that it is God who has given me all of the abilities and gifts to accomplish these things.

One of my dear friends in ministry, Paul Stark, is one of my greatest supports. He and I have helped each other through many spiritual battles. Paul is a constant encouragement when I want to quit. In fact, we have both talked each other out of quitting on several occasions. We have come to believe that in ministry, if you do not feel like quitting at least once a week, you're not doing it right. For me, it has been incredibly helpful to have someone in the ditch with me who deeply understands the ditch. He doesn't always tell me what I want to hear, but instead he forces me to think differently about the situation and refuses to let me take the easy way out.

As the Scriptures say – this is a spiritual battle, and Satan attacks those who serve the Lord – but **"the one who is in you is greater than the one who is in the world"** (1 John 4:4). This verse has always given me comfort and hope, because no matter how deep or difficult a "ditch" we face in our lives, Jesus is greater. This verse acknowledges that the world is a tough adversary. The world will beat us down and overwhelm us at times with its "greatness." But greater is He! We can also take comfort in the fact that Jesus places other people in the "ditch" alongside us to support, encourage and love us. No one has to go through it alone. And while what happens in the ditch may stay in the ditch – the valuable insights and lessons that we gain from spending time in the ditch will last a lifetime.

Questions for Reflection and Discussion

1. What "ditches" have you been in?

2. Who have you been with in the "ditch?" What did you learn from each other?

3. Who would you want to dig a ditch with? Why?

4. What do you do when you feel like quitting your ministry?

You Need to Go

Leaving – it's one of the hardest things in life to do. But at times, it's necessary. It can be stressful, exciting, and scary – all at the same time. You may find you are constantly second-guessing yourself, wondering if you're really doing the right thing. It's just so hard to say good-bye sometimes! And with every move comes a sense of loss and mourning for what is left behind, even if it's just a sense of familiarity.

Jesus talked about the need to leave at times, whether it be for a short while – **"Come with me by yourselves to a quiet place and get some rest"** (Mark 10:7) – or permanently – **"For this reason a man will leave his father and mother and be united to his wife"** (Mark 6:31). Even when it's a spiritual decision to leave, and we receive wise counsel from others pointing to what God is clearly telling us, there is often a little bit of doubt lingering in our mind. Maybe it's doubt the size of a mustard seed!

Could it be a good thing that we have a little bit of doubt? Without doubt, can we ever really come to understand what faith is all about? By definition, faith is belief that is not based on proof. In the absence of hard evidence, God uses our struggles with doubt to help us learn, over time, to trust Him and have faith in Him. On the other hand, people who are afraid to have any degree of doubt often end up rejecting God because they are yearning for something concrete and logical that does *not* require a trusting heart. As we mature as Christians, doubts diminish and our faith increases. But as we mature, God also asks us to expand our horizons, and so it's not surprising that we might again be challenged by doubts about what lies just over the next hill. The important thing is to keep walking hand in hand with Jesus, and not allow doubts to stand in our way.

Isn't it interesting that God Himself spoke to Moses from a burning bush – and yet Moses *still* had doubts (Exodus 3:1-12)? Moses had a pretty good gig going as a shepherd. Leaving that life behind meant a lot more work and headaches. But when God calls you to go – you need to go!

I am one of those odd people who loves being selected for jury duty. I get to meet new people. The government buys me lunch. I get to take days off from work. I get to sit there and feel important and pretend I understand the law. What's not to love? I had jury duty in 2011, and the defense lawyer was attempting to explain to the jurors what "beyond a reasonable doubt" means. Many of us have heard this term on *Law and Order* or read it in John Grisham novels. But do we really know what it means? The attorney explained it as the feeling of certainty we often have when we ask someone to marry us, or when we accept a marriage proposal, or when we buy a car or house. He argued that we do these things with great excitement when we are confident in the outcome, i.e., when we have a confidence that is "beyond a reasonable doubt." It's not the absence of *all* doubt. Nevertheless, we proceed anyway because the doubts are overshadowed by everything else we are presented with. In a court of law, the doubts are outweighed by legal evidence. So if we apply this same concept to our spiritual lives, this is what it means: When we allow our doubts to be overshadowed by God's overwhelming grace, then we can proceed with a confidence and excitement that may at times defy logic.

Pastor Andy Stanley argues in his book *Next Generation Leader* that we should move forward when we have 80% certainty. Does the remaining 20% doubt seem like reasonable doubt to you? While every circumstance is unique, and we all have different comfort levels when it comes to this kind of thing, the point is that we should not just sit on our hands and wait for 100% certainty when it comes to making a decision, even when it's a decision that impacts our ministry. It can be scary, but I encourage you to take reasonable risks in your missional life. Think of it this way: If you don't take risks that are inherent with change, then you are choosing to take the risk of becoming inactive or stagnant. And remember that no matter how bumpy the ride gets, or how far off our original "track" we might get, God is always in control and **"in all things God works for the good of those who love him"** (Romans 8:28).

My wife and I like to say that we are living proof that God exists, because nobody leaves Hawaii unless God tells them to! And I will fully admit that there are some days when I come home from a long day at work and think – man – we should have just stayed in Hawaii! Plus, it just so happens that we left Hawaii six months after my wife's parents moved back there! We struggled with uncertainty as we prayed and sought counsel about whether God was calling us to move. Needless to say, it was a stressful time for us. By the mercy and grace of God, we are still married!

Even though we were hesitant to go there originally in 2001, leaving Southern California in 2009 was just as difficult for us. We were serving a great church in Orange where my position provided me with the two things I crave most in ministry: freedom and challenge. I loved my job at St. Paul's and I treasured the wisdom, friendships, and support of my coworkers. We had so many wonderful friends – as did our children. We had a beautiful home that we had put plenty of sweat equity into. In fact, when I told Christy that Concordia Texas wanted to fly us out for a visit, she was in the middle of painting the master bathroom thinking – *I'm never leaving this house!* God has a wonderful sense of humor! Christy said it best when she said, "We're living the dream!" But God told us to go – and even though we weren't 100% sure – we had to go!

Interestingly, when leaving Hawaii and California, both times I had a crucial conversation with one of the students involved in my ministry. I thank God that I have people in my life that love me and know me well enough to tell me the difficult truth. In Hawaii, it was Jenna. I arrived during her eighth grade year, and as I introduced myself to her she responded with, "My dog's name is Jake." And in the four years I was there, she had grown into an incredible leader. She completely grasped the vision of the ministry, was constantly inviting her friends to youth activities, and was the top student leader of our ministry. The week after it was announced that I received a call to Orange, California, she came into my office, closed the door, starting crying – very hard, mind you – and said, "I don't want you to go – but you need to go. It's the best thing for you and Christy." It was the end of her junior year of high school. She was so excited about becoming a senior, and she really wanted me there to help her prepare for life after high school. But she selflessly heard the call for us, and told us the honest truth.

In Orange, California, it was Matt. We had received the call to Concordia Texas, and Matt told me straight up that it was time to go as well. No tears, but sorrow and honesty. He said that the opportunity to go to Texas and train future church workers was one I had to take, and one that he felt God had been preparing me for with all of my years of ministry experience. It was his senior year of high school, and he too was thinking selflessly. He could see the bigger picture of ministry. It is important to note that Jenna and Matt were not adults, mentors, or people who would benefit in any way from my leaving. In fact, their lives became more difficult without me there. But they understood the vision of changing the world for Jesus, and they knew that I had to go.

Is there somewhere you have to go? Do you have people in your life who will tell you the honest, but difficult truth? Yes, there will be doubt. There will be difficulty and hardship. Going is not easy, but if God calls you to go – you need to go! Going is an important part of living life as a mission trip. In fact, many Greek language scholars argue that the tense of **"go"** in The Great Commission (Matthew 28:16-20) is incorrect in most translations. Verse 19 starts: **"Therefore go and make disciples…"** They argue that a better translation is: "Therefore in your going make disciples…" Did you catch the difference? It isn't just "go" – to arrive at a destination and then start our work – it is "in your going" – to work continually as we keep moving from one adventure to the next, which God has planned for us. We will never fully realize all that God has planned for us until we *go*!

Questions for Reflection and Discussion

1. In your past, have you ever known that you needed to leave, but you really didn't want to? How did you handle it?

2. What percent certainty do you feel you need before you make a decision? Why? Do you think this percentage is higher or lower than most people?

3. Is it usually easier for you to go, or to stay? Why?

4. Matthew 28:17 reminds us that some of the followers of Jesus still doubted – even after they had seen Him resurrected! What does that say about our doubts?

Top Ten Ways to Ruin a Mission Trip – #10 and #9

#10

Focus Only on Church-y Stuff

Let me define "church-y" stuff as anything related to a physical church building. Most of us are comfortable with the concept that the church isn't the building – it's the people. And yet, all too often, we focus on church as a physical place: *Let's go to church. We're meeting at church. The church is on the corner of Main Street and 5th.* If you want to limit your missional life, put all your energy into bringing people into the church instead of bringing the church to the people!

One of my favorite assignments in my Witness and Evangelism class is to require students to do a "random act of kindness." They are to provide significant help to a complete stranger. The trick is that they are not to explain why they are doing this or talk about faith in any way – unless asked. It's a way to *live* the Gospel instead of just *speaking* the Gospel. I really enjoy reading the finished assignments and hearing about what each student chose to do, and it is rewarding and fun to process with them what they experienced.

One of my students, on a very rare snowy day in Austin, spent an hour in the parking lot of the local grocery store cleaning the snow off of the windshields of cars. She got into multiple conversations with people who asked her why she was doing this. She received many kind words, brought big smiles to several faces, and got plenty of thank-yous. However, one response stood out. One particular woman asked her why she was doing this, and my student replied that she was studying to be in ministry and this was a service to bless people. The recipient of this grace act was very impressed and said, "I didn't know ministers ever went outside of the church."

Wow! That response will haunt me forever. We have somehow communicated to the world that only church-y stuff is important for "ministers." Sometimes in your mission, you will paint a house, dig a ditch, play with a kid, clean up trash, visit with the lonely, etc., and these seemingly "nonsacred" acts can show the love, mercy, and grace of Jesus Christ as much as any sermon or hymn!

Church-y things certainly have their place, but in order to be a missionary and reach people where they are, we cannot focus on them. The idea that some things are only secular while others are only sacred is not a Biblical concept. God is the creator of all things, which means everything can be rightly viewed from a spiritual perspective and can be used to glorify God! Perhaps the most important thing a missionary can do is show people the sacred aspects in the things of the world that they perceive to be secular.

#9

Point Out Mistakes

Mission trips are full of mistakes – big ones and small ones. Now, some of these mistakes do need to be pointed out. If a decision or action is going to seriously hurt someone, we should speak up immediately! Yet, most of the time, what we perceive to be "mistakes" are usually just differences of opinion. Pointing them out and trying to correct them can lead to relationship issues if dealt with improperly.

There are three important parts to this concept. The first is pointing out the mistakes of team members. If you want to damage your mission trip experience, draw attention to every mistake you think every team member makes. This could also be an effective way to exert some authority and establish yourself as higher than they are in the "pecking order." (I hope you can tell I'm being sarcastic!)

Team members come from a variety of different backgrounds and have mixed levels of experience. This diversity should be viewed as a very positive thing – because it provides an opportunity for everyone to learn things from one another. Besides, short-term mission trips are, well, short. So, there is only so much time to "fix" our fellow team members! Instead of looking at others with a critical eye, we should try to be more tolerant and adaptable when it comes to working with others on a mission trip.

Let's take a look at Matthew chapter 18 and see what Jesus has to say about resolving conflict. He says, **"If your brother sins against you…"** (verse 15). Notice several key words here. "Sins" is perhaps the most important one. It does not say annoys, pesters, or drives you crazy. It says *sins*. At least in my experience, the mistakes I usually see made by my team members are more annoyances than actual sins. I would even go so far as to say that when my team member annoys me, the sin is actually mine and not theirs, because I am not loving them the way they deserve to be loved as a child of God!

Also in verse 15, notice the very first word of the sentence – "if." *If* your brother sins against you – not *when* your brother sins against you. There is great hope in these words of Jesus that the Christian community would be different than the communities of the world. In the world, people will be sinning against each other; it's just a matter of when. But in this new community – this new creation – what if we loved each other the way Jesus loves us? What if we took mercy and grace seriously, by applying it more consistently to each other? What if we were different? People might even be attracted to us because of our unique and radical love!

The second part of dealing with "mistakes" is when we point out the errors of our own mission team leaders. Leading is hard. It takes endurance and integrity. While leaders are certainly not perfect, the good ones consistently put the needs of their followers ahead of their own. Highlighting mistakes of leaders can hurt their credibility – not only with the team but also with the local people you are trying to minister to. This can certainly damage your mission! Perhaps the key is to lean toward the old leadership adage of "Praise in public; criticize in private." (Vince Lombardi)

The final part I'd like to discuss is when we point out the mistakes of the local, indigenous leaders. We need to respect their leadership and authority the same way we would expect visitors to respect our knowledge and decisions when they come to our home. I've seen this to be especially harmful when it comes to building projects.

One of the things I love about Habitat for Humanity International is they build structures in the local style. This usually means that you can leave your hammer at home – because most cultures don't build with wood and nails! It may not always be the most efficient or effective building style from our American point of view – but it's the local style! I've seen so many well-meaning people come in and criticize the local builders – for example, experienced construction workers showing them the "right way" to do something. This can ruin the relationship with the local people and damage the valuable opportunity to share the Gospel! Just because it's different doesn't mean it's *wrong*. Just because you wouldn't do it that way doesn't mean that others can't.

I'm not trying to say that it's always wrong to offer a constructive suggestion. Sometimes we may have valuable input to share. However, any suggestion about how to do something differently needs to be done *after* a firm relationship has been established. My favorite thing to do when I get to a new build site is to ask for the toughest, worst job – the one that nobody in their right mind would want to do. There has yet to be a lack of this kind of work! This philosophy has led to my doing a variety of unpleasant jobs – everything from digging nine foot deep ditches to working on the roof in blazing heat and with spotty ladders.

In Brazil, the job that nobody else wanted to do was mix cement. I didn't mind doing this job, especially this time because instead of mixing it by hand, we had a big old diesel cement mixer! However, I noticed that their post-mixing method struck me as a little inefficient. We made cement in the mixer, dumped it on the ground, and then shoveled it into wheelbarrows to be moved to the places it was needed. It was very hard work, in very extreme heat. It did seem like there was a needless step in the process. But instead of jumping in to correct their techniques, I focused on relationships and had a great time getting to know the masons. I helped them with the cement for four days straight.

On the fifth day, I felt we had bonded enough that I could make a suggestion that just might improve the overall operation. I suggested that instead of dumping the cement on the ground, we could dump it right into the wheelbarrows and save a step. They loved it! You would have thought I invented sliced bread or Velcro®! They thought this was just about the best idea ever. But, I am convinced that if I had suggested a change to their system earlier in the week, without first establishing a relationship, it could have damaged the relationship we had with them. If you do not want to ruin your mission, focus on building relationships and communicating Jesus, not on pointing out mistakes!

Personal Mission Perspective

Only in a Ditch
by Amanda White

I had been on other mission trips before we went to El
Salvador in the summer of 2010, but I hadn't yet been on a
trip with Jake Youmans. I quickly learned that Jake did
mission trips differently. It was about the people, it was about
Jesus, and it was about serving. One of my biggest takeaways
– and my advice for anyone planning to go on a mission trip –
is to pick the hardest, dirtiest, least wanted job and volunteer
happily!

In El Salvador, we were serving with Habitat for Humanity.
There were lots of jobs to be done: painting, soil-sifting,
shoveling, wheelbarrowing, weeding, and.... ditch-digging.
Immediately, Jake says, "I'll dig the ditch!" I follow naively,
not knowing this "ditch" is more like a 6 foot well.

What we were rewarded with was well worth it. Not only did
we dig the dang thing, we also spent many hours sharing
stories of ministry, family, life, and how they all work in
harmony (and sometimes don't). The struggle of digging a
huge hole was paired with stories of struggle with my
relationship with my dad. This sharing probably wouldn't
have happened if we were not in a ditch in El Salvador.

When we got near the end of the hole, one of us had to be digging and the other had to lift buckets of soil out of the hole. And when we would switch off, one would lower a ladder into the hole for the other. That ladder was the only way to get out. In this moment, I could only think of how it is like God's relationship with us. He lets us dig ourselves deep sometimes, but He is always there with a ladder to help us out. We are never alone.

In the end, I realized so much more reward comes from doing the dirty, hard, unwanted jobs. It builds relationships. No doubt God works while we paint and weed as well, but we put ourselves in a more vulnerable place when we do something we think we can't. God moves powerfully in us because we put our trust in Him. That's the thing about missions – we have to trust that God will bridge the gap of culture and language, and overcome our barriers. And He always does.

· · · · ·

Amanda White has a passion for Christ and His work in the hearts of students. She has always had a heart for missions, but it wasn't until after her graduation from Concordia Texas and the DCE program that she felt the call to long-term missions. In January 2014, God willing, Amanda will travel with The World Race to serve Jesus in 11 countries in 11 months!

Judea

Introduction to Judea

Judea is the name given to the southern kingdom of Israel. While there is a great deal of history leading up to how we got two kingdoms of Israel, the basic idea is that after King Solomon, author of the book of Proverbs and heir to King David, the kingdom was divided into two parts: the north and the south. The north kept the name Israel while the south went by the name Judea. The common name of "Jew" is actually taken from the name Judea.

The area of Judea is named after the dominant tribe of the south – Judah. The tribe derived its name from the fourth son of the patriarch Jacob (whose name God changed to Israel – Genesis 35:10) and Leah. The meaning of the name Judah is "praise and thanks." Several of the Biblical cities that you have heard of – Jerusalem, Bethany, and that little town of Bethlehem – are located within the area known as Judea. The geographical area is certainly larger than a city, and in our North American context, it could be comparable to a "state." However, the metaphorical meaning of Judea is so much more.

Metaphorically, I want us to think of Judea as people who are not Christian but are otherwise similar to us. Judeans are, for whatever reasons, not connected to Jesus Christ as Lord and Savior. Maybe they are not involved in church because no one invited them. Maybe they have prioritized worldly things over God. Maybe they are down on their luck and need a little help to get back on their feet. Maybe a tragedy or a painful past has caused them to feel separated from God. Whatever their reasons may be, God just may use you to help them see

Jesus! Judea could be across the country, or even across the street. Let's explore how we can be missional in Judea.

Uncle Lester

One way you can encounter Judea is through a local homeless shelter. Fortunately (or unfortunately, based on your point of view), nearly every community in the country has some kind of homeless ministry. I have been blessed to visit and work with a wide variety of homeless shelters all over the world. A shelter in Santa Ana, California provides free legal assistance to help guests get back on their feet. A facility in New Zealand includes a worship experience with a meal. A shelter in Austin, Texas doesn't wait for people to come to them – they go into the alleyways and streets to distribute boxed lunches to the needy. A facility in Anchorage, Alaska provides not only a warm meal but also warm clothes, which can make the difference between life and death in the winter on the streets of Anchorage. All of these ministries, and countless more like them, take the mission of serving the less fortunate very seriously! I'm not sure where God has placed you right now, but as you look to live life as a mission trip, I would almost guarantee there is some kind of homeless ministry in your area that would be very grateful for your assistance.

Perhaps my favorite homeless ministry is River of Life Mission in Honolulu, Hawaii. Situated in Chinatown, right downtown, they serve three meals a day, seven days a week, 365 days a year. The nightly dinner includes a worship experience provided by local partnering churches. Bibles are readily available for anyone who would like one. (On my last trip there, I had the privilege of handing out several Bibles to folks who asked for them.) There are shower facilities for those who want to get cleaned up. They have secondhand clothes neatly sorted and laid out, available for those who need them. They have a housing referral ministry to help folks get off the streets. They have specific programs to help the addicted kick their destructive habits. And the most fascinating part for me is that the majority of employees and volunteers are "graduates" of River of Life. It is a powerful and humbling experience to serve our guests alongside coworkers who were recently guests themselves, but by the grace and mercy of God have gotten their lives back on track. River of Life even has a chocolate factory (Chocolate on a Mission) that helps them raise the funds needed to provide all of these services! It's a very impressive place!

On a recent trip to help out at the mission, the five of us in our group signed in and were immediately given responsibilities. Two of my students were assigned to work in the dining room and distribute meals to the guests. The rest of us were sent to the kitchen, where we met Uncle Lester. Now, almost every homeless shelter I've ever served at has an "Uncle Lester." Uncle Lester has been serving at River of Life longer than anyone can remember. He is the boss. He is the dictator of all that happens in the kitchen – oh, excuse me – all that happens in *his* kitchen! He loves to pick on new volunteers, especially the leaders of groups that come to serve. Uncle Lester does not speak. He has the ability to speak, but instead chooses to communicate with grunts, stares, and head motions. He is ageless. I honestly cannot even guess how old he is. But as strange as it may sound, I love working with the "Uncle Lester" types. And again, just about every shelter has one! If you can break through their shell, they always have incredible stories!

Uncle Lester assigned the other two students in my group to cooking duty. But he took one look at me, sized me up and down, and I could tell that I was in trouble. He grunted and motioned to three rows of boxes stacked five feet high in a back room with nothing else in it. I went over to these boxes and realized they were full of onions. He made it clear, in his own unique Uncle Lester way, that I was to chop up all of these onions. Now, for this story to really make sense, you have to know that I despise onions. I *loathe* onions. They are by far my least favorite food in the world. Even people who barely know me seem to understand this about me, and yet somehow Uncle Lester presented me with my ultimate Kryptonite.

My philosophy on a mission experience is simple – anything for Jesus! So I chopped. And I chopped. And I chopped. From 8 A.M. till noon, I chopped. Without taking a break, without any complaint, I chopped. Please don't think I enjoyed it. I hated every single second of it! But I did it with a smile, humming Jesus songs while I chopped. I honestly cannot remember ever dicing up *one* onion in my life – let alone *boxes* of them! The smell was overpowering, and before long, my eyes started stinging and tearing up. In fact, it became harder and harder to keep my eyes open to see what I was doing, and I began to wonder how many fingers I would have left after I was done. I knew my hands would probably reek of onions for the rest of my life, as the distinctive odor seemed to penetrate the skin and work its way into my DNA like a nasty parasite. (See, I *told* you I hate onions!)

Throughout the morning, Uncle Lester would come to check on me – not saying a word, positively or negatively – but he would check. I assume the checks were to make sure I was still working!

At 12 noon sharp, Uncle Lester walked back into my work area and scrutinized my work more closely than he had before. At that point, I only had two boxes of onions left. Without saying a word, he picked up those boxes and handed them to me. Then it happened. He *spoke*. He turned his back to me, started walking out the door, and said: "Follow me."

I did exactly that. I did think it was interesting that the first words he spoke to me were also the first words Jesus spoke to his disciples (Matthew 4:19), but I didn't have time to process it. I just followed him. We left the kitchen and then the facility. We started to wander through Chinatown, down some streets and a few alleys. I felt a little bit like Indiana Jones – but certainly looked more like Indiana Jones's sidekick who's the first to die! After a dozen or so blocks, we wandered into a farmer's market-type store front. And it happened. Lester spoke *more* than two words! But – not to me. He offered the onions to the woman who ran the shop. She graciously accepted, they exchanged pleasantries, and off Lester and I went.

As we walked back to the mission, Lester finally started talking to me. He told me that the mission had a relationship with that particular store, and they shared vegetables with each other whenever they had extras. This is when it got really good, because I had twelve blocks to learn his story. Lester had been working at the mission for 15 years. He was never homeless or abused or addicted to anything. He was in construction – as a stone mason. One day, he got hurt on the job and couldn't work anymore. He sat around his house for months doing absolutely nothing but watching TV and feeling sorry for himself. But then he finally realized that he had been given the gift of time, and even though he could no longer do construction, he could still do something construc*tive*.

So he telephoned about half a dozen local ministries to see if they could use a volunteer. River of Life Mission was the first to call him back, and they invited him to come down and volunteer the following day. And he's been at the mission every day since! About eight years ago, he was asked to run the kitchen. He's still a volunteer, but he's there helping out more often than many of the full-time employees.

Lester has no formal training as a cook – his only training is as a mason – but he feeds thousands of people a week! He talked to me about his faith journey and how much he's grown while serving at River of Life. He did not start working at the mission because of his faith, but his faith is now what brings him back every morning. He gets to see lives changed every day, and he is privileged to work with so many amazing people from all over the world, even though he himself has never left the island of Oahu.

What a fascinating human being! What a selfless servant of Jesus! I had a thousand questions for him and wanted to become his best friend, but I only had about a block and a half left. I figured that once we entered back inside the mission, Lester would have to stop talking to me again. I really only had time for one question. So I asked him, "Lester, which of Jesus' words mean the most to you?" (I think this is a more fun way to ask: "What's your favorite Bible verse?") **"Follow me, and I will make you fishers of men"** (cf. Matthew 4:19) Lester replied, without having to think about it. "I was a mason. I have no cooking skills. I was a builder, but now I 'build' meals for people who need them. Everything I do is about being a follower of Jesus." And after watching him for several days, his statement was no exaggeration. I do not recall ever witnessing a more selfless servant. He personally has dropped everything to follow Jesus!

Now that I have had the time to process Uncle Lester telling me to "follow him," it is interesting to me that I followed him without hesitation through the streets of Chinatown. I didn't really know him at the time. I had seen him work, and I had heard plenty about him, but didn't *know* him. Yet when he said, "follow me," I followed. I had no idea where he was taking me, but I didn't question or doubt. I just left everything and followed him.

· · · · ·

In the book of Matthew, there are four different times when Jesus calls specific people to follow Him. The first, and perhaps the most famous, is when He's talking to Peter, Andrew, James, and John as they are fishing in chapter 4. **"'Come, follow me,' Jesus said, 'and I will make you fishers of men'"** (verse 19, NIV 1984). Their response? They left everything and followed Him.

In Matthew chapter 8, one of Jesus' disciples says: **"Lord, first let me go and bury my father"** (verse 21). Jesus' response? **"Follow me"** (verse 22). And then Jesus and his disciples got into the boat and were off on their next adventure.

In Matthew chapter 9, Jesus first encounters Matthew, the actual author of the book that bears his name. Matthew was a tax collector, very important and very busy. Jesus encounters him and says: **"Follow me"** (verse 9). Matthew leaves his tax stand and immediately follows Jesus. You can see the recurring theme. Jesus calls – people follow. And they drop everything when they go. Neither employment nor family commitments take priority over Jesus.

But then a few chapters later, in Matthew 19, Jesus has a different encounter – this time with someone who's been called the "Rich Young Ruler." This man asks Jesus what he must do to inherit eternal life. Jesus tells him to give everything he owns to the poor and follow Him. And the man's response? He walks away sad, because he was very wealthy. He couldn't follow Jesus because he couldn't drop everything. For him, his material, earthly things took priority over Jesus and the eternal life He brings.

What does following Jesus mean to you? Like Uncle Lester, Jesus may call you to something you never expected, or that you feel you have no training or preparation for. But He has equipped you for it nonetheless. What do you have to "drop" to truly follow Jesus the way you have been called? Is there something in your life that is taking priority over Jesus? Are you unwilling to leave certain things behind? These are difficult but crucial questions we each must ask ourselves as we look to view life as a mission trip.

I finally got Lester to smile at me – when I told him I was leaving! I asked for a picture with him and he graciously accepted. He even smiled in the picture! Thank God for the Uncle Lesters in our life who boldly follow Jesus in the way they have been called!

Questions for Reflection and Discussion

1. How have you heard Jesus say, "Follow Me?"

2. Which of Jesus' words mean the most to you? Why?

3. What are some ways you can volunteer your time, skills, and compassion to help others in need?

Quilts

I have a denim quilt that my grandmother made for me. She gave it to me when I first headed off to college. She made it by hand, and her love is in every single stitch of that quilt. I have gotten quite a bit of use out of it over the years. It was what I used as my main blanket on my bed until I got married. And now it's what we use when we cuddle on the couch as we read or watch television. I love that quilt, and every time I see it I think about my amazing grandmother. She's the smartest and most beautiful woman in the world. She lived through the Great Depression and World War II. She raised four kids, and has gotten to enjoy 16 grandchildren and eight great grandchildren (so far!). At the ripe old age of 84 ½, she now spends much of her time in a wheelchair, but her mind is as sharp as ever. She lost the love of her life – my grandfather – in January 2011. Since then, she has been living alone for the first time in her life! I am amazed by her and love her dearly. The quilt she made for me is a constant reminder of her love for me!

I have actually learned quite a bit more about quilts recently, as my little brother Nathan has joined the quilting group at his church. It's a flock of ladies in their sixties or older – and a 32-year-old man! He loves interacting with the ladies. They feed him rather well, as you can imagine! And he enjoys the creative process of making a quilt. I will admit that when I first heard he was a quilter, I made fun of him… a little… but

I'm starting to appreciate the beauty of it all. (I've been looking for a bumper sticker for Nathan that says "Quilt or Die" – but haven't found one yet.)

Also, my wife Christy's brother Steven recently married Alicia, who is a professional quilter. Her company is called Stitch-a-Story, and she uses quilts as a means to tell people's stories. She has made quilts from T-shirts collected on a family vacation. She has made quilts out of the clothes of a loved one who has passed away. Families greatly cherish these keepsakes, as you can imagine! Alicia believes every quilt can tell a story.

On a trip to Buffalo, New York, I worshipped at a church just outside the city on what happened to be their "Quilt Dedication Sunday." Having a newfound appreciation for quilts, I was very excited to see what they would do on this special day. The pews were covered with quilts, with two or three draped over every pew. There must have been over 200 quilts altogether! The place looked very impressive. The quilts were all different colors and patterns. No two looked alike. We prayed over the quilts, asking God to bless the people who would be receiving them.

After worship, I went up to one of the little old ladies who had made some of the quilts and thanked her for her ministry. We engaged in some pleasant small talk, as it was the kind of church where everyone knew I was a visitor. Then I asked her, "Where are you going to send all of these quilts?"

"We live in Buffalo," she replied with a big smile.

"Yes, I know – this is my first time visiting here. But where are you going to send the quilts?"

"We live in Buffalo," she said again, still smiling. I figured she didn't fully understand my question.

"I realize that," I said, trying very hard not to sound frustrated. So I asked again – "But *where* are you sending the quilts?"

"We live in Buffalo," she said again, ever so politely.

Okay, you said that a few times now, I thought. So this time I decided to give her some options. Maybe a multiple choice question would help her answer my missional question. "Are you going to send the quilts to Africa? Or maybe to Asia? Or to South America? Where are you sending the quilts?"

"Africa? I'm not sure people in Africa need quilts, dear. We're sending them to Buffalo. There is a shelter right downtown that we have been working with for years. Every year after the Quilt Dedication, we give them our entire supply to distribute to people who need some help right here in town."

So, she understood my question the entire time! It turns out that I was the one who didn't fully understand. Yes, it makes perfect sense – people need help in Buffalo – and who better to help them than the people who live in… Buffalo! Simply put, being missional in Judea means reaching out to people in your own community who are like you – people who have similar needs as you do. And while I have not yet experienced a true Buffalo winter, I think it's safe to say that everyone who lives in Buffalo needs a good warm quilt! Especially one that was made with love and care by the folks right here in town!

I didn't get to meet any of the people who received these quilts, but I would bet that they all loved their beautiful handmade gift. And the amazing thing about giving a quilt is that you're not just giving a blanket – you're also giving a story! A story of someone who saw a simple need – the need for a warm blanket – and responded lavishly with an intricate and exquisite quilt. A story of a God whose love compelled someone to spend countless hours creating a quilt that they themselves would never get to use, but would instead be given to someone they didn't even know. A story of a group of dedicated, loving people working together to improve the lives of others – both physically and emotionally. The story of Jesus was communicated through every single one of those quilts that we dedicated that Sunday!

· · · · ·

Jesus told stories everywhere He went. This was even prophesied about Him in the Old Testament: **"My people, hear my teaching; listen to the words of my mouth. I will open my mouth with a parable; I will utter hidden things, things from of old – things we have heard and known, things our ancestors have told us."** (Psalm 78:1-3) I often picture Jesus walking around, enjoying the handiwork of His creation – birds, flowers, trees, etc. – prompting Him to include these things in His parables as He taught about the Kingdom of God. Stories are the oldest form of communication and education. They are such a basic and innate part of our lives. In fact, we each have our very own unique life story, which is similar to a "quilt" pieced together from all the people, events, emotions, and special memories we hold dear.

When we give of ourselves – our time, our resources, our talents – to help someone else, we are sharing part of our own unique story with them. There has to be a reason for what we do. Our Story is Jesus, risen Lord, and Savior of the world. And while a quilt will bless someone else for a time, that Story of Jesus will bless them for *all* time!

Questions for Reflection and Discussion

1. What are some of the ways that you share your personal story with others?

2. When you think of the mission field, do you tend to think of it as being far away or nearby? Why?

3. What could you collect and give away in your local community?

Inspiration

What inspires you? We would not do the things we do without some kind of inspiration. In training future church workers, I love to ask them who or what inspired them to go into ministry. Everyone has a story, and those stories are always fascinating and usually very personal. Some of the motivating factors are "negative" – where we do not want anyone else to experience the pain and difficulty we went through. Some are "positive" – where we want others to be blessed in the same way we have been, or perhaps we have aspirations to be just like our mentor who inspired us. But there is always an inspiration!

I'll always remember a youth minister we met in New Zealand. She was an Australian who was serving for two years in a small church on the southern tip of the North Island. She told me she went into ministry because a group of Americans had visited and led a Youth Night at her home church when she was in high school. She can't remember any of their names and she never connected with any of them again – but the event changed her life forever. She was so inspired by people traveling so far and spending so much money just to tell her about the love of Jesus. His love felt real to her for the first time that night because someone had sacrificed their time and resources to make sure others knew. She said she wanted to inspire people in the same way, and that's why she left her home and came to minister in New

Zealand. Think about the power of mission work! Lives change, even when we are not aware of it!

Another good example is the second-career pastor I once met who went to seminary when his own kids were teenagers. He grew up Catholic and his wife used to be Baptist, but they both drifted away from religion. It just so happened that their children became really good friends with some kids who went to the local Lutheran church. At the time, he and his wife had no idea what a Lutheran was, but the idea of their kids doing something constructive appealed to them. Their kids became involved in church activities, and soon the kids were dragging their mom and dad to church as well. It didn't take long for both mom and dad to get connected and become volunteers in the youth program. They took the kids to youth gatherings and mission trips, and invested their lives in them. Within a year, the whole family was inspired to go into ministry, with dad enrolling in a Lutheran seminary. The kids inspired the parents!

Obviously, I could tell many other stories, but I chose these two to illustrate the power of living a missional life, both at home and far from home. We all have the God-given potential to inspire others – not only the people closest to us, but also people we may never see again. Traveling around the world to share Jesus, with all the sacrifices it entails, is inspiring. Going next door to share your faith with your neighbor, with all the risks involved, is inspiring. Inviting your mom/dad/daughter/son to church is inspiring – and might be the most challenging of all! We don't always know how (or even if) our actions will reach the heart of a particular person, but certainly there is great potential to inspire when we live life as a mission trip!

. . . . .

John the Baptist has always intrigued me – and not just because of his choices of outfit and diet (Matthew 3:4). He's the last in the line of the prophets (Matthew 11:13). Most scholars believe he's a cousin of Jesus. He even had the awe-inducing opportunity to baptize Jesus Himself (Matthew 3:13-15)! John dedicated his life to ministry and service. Yet, despite all he had seen and heard, he still struggled with doubt.

John spent a good deal of time in prison – and was eventually killed by King Herod (Matthew 14:1-12). Can you imagine how confusing it must have been for John the Baptist to be stuck in prison? This was the guy who had the honor of baptizing Jesus. He had heard the voice of God from heaven and had seen the Holy Spirit descend like a dove and land on Jesus (Matthew 3:16-17). He seemed so confident in the beginning about who Jesus was (John 1:29-36). But we can also imagine John sitting miserably in prison, wondering: *Why isn't Jesus getting me out? There is no way He's going to let me die in prison, right?* His doubt is evident in the message that John sent to Jesus from prison: **"Are you the one who is to come, or should we expect someone else?"** (Matthew 11:3) Can you hear the hopelessness in his words? These are the last words we have from the great prophet. Jesus even said there was no man greater than John (Matthew 11:11) – and these are John's last recorded words.

Even John the Baptist doubted! His faith was strong when things were going well, but he began to doubt when circumstances were difficult and things weren't happening the way he expected. John eventually is beheaded in Matthew chapter 14. Was John still wondering if he had put his hope in the wrong person? Was he pondering if he should be looking for a bigger, better messiah – maybe one that would get him out of prison? Actually, I don't think John was thinking such thoughts by the time of his death because if you read Jesus' response to John's question, His words dispel all such doubts. (And I do believe Jesus' words got through to John in time because Jesus Himself directs: **"...report to John..."** (Matthew 11:4), and when Jesus gives an order such as this, it's as good as done (Ephesians 2:10)!)

Jesus told John's disciples:

> **Go back and report to John what you hear and see: The blind receive sight, the lame walk, those who have leprosy are cleansed, the deaf hear, the dead are raised, and the good news is proclaimed to the poor. Blessed is anyone who does not stumble on account of me.** (Matthew 11:4-6)

When questioned on His identity, the proof that Jesus gives is that people's lives have been transformed by Him. There is no bigger inspiration than a changed life. And He reminds John's disciples that they have heard and seen these things for themselves. In addition to Jesus' words, they have experienced it with their own God-given senses!

Have you personally experienced a changed life? Perhaps you have gone through dramatic changes, positive or negative, that continue to inspire you to move forward with Christ. But even small, simple changes can be profound when we look at them through the lens of the biggest change – the transformation from death to life – that all believers experience in Jesus.

Living life as a mission trip is inspiring, and all of us – regardless of skill or giftedness – have the opportunity to inspire others. You may never know who or exactly how you inspire, but pray that God will use you as an inspiration. And when you pray that prayer, be prepared to be challenged and changed yourself!

Questions for Reflection and Discussion

1. Think of a person who has inspired you greatly in your life. Have you ever told them how much of a difference they have made? If not, how can you thank them in some way?

2. Do you feel like you are an inspiration to other people? Why or why not?

3. What kinds of things do you find most inspiring in your faith life? Why?

4. What is your greatest inspiration for sharing Jesus with others?

The Eulogy

The phone rang innocently enough. My mom told me I had a phone call, which I thought was a little odd because I had only been home for Christmas break for a few days. It was my senior year of college, and I certainly needed the time at home to relax. The voice on the other end of the phone was not instantly familiar to me. It turned out to be the mother of my good friend from high school – Sheila. This was even more odd, because even though I loved Sheila dearly, we had not kept in touch very much since we finished high school. But I was excited to hear from her family, thinking maybe she was inviting me to a party or something during the break.

What her mother said to me next completely floored me.

"Sheila's dead."

It sounded so cold, so unbelievable. She didn't soften the blow in any way. She just came right out and said it.

"Whaaaaat?! How?!" I felt my heart jump into my throat and my stomach sink, both at the same time.

It turns out that Sheila – this beautiful, 23-year-old, full of life, master's student – was driving back home from school in Utah when she was involved in a fatal car accident. And now she was dead. I was in absolute shock. I didn't know what to say or how to react. I just stood there holding the phone up to my ear, feeling completely detached from reality.

Sheila's mom continued. "I'm calling because I was wondering if you would give a eulogy."

"Of course!" I said, without even thinking about it. I had never given one before, but I was happy to help Sheila's family in any way I could.

Her requests were not done. "And could you ask your pastor to do the funeral?" she asked.

"Of course! I'm sure he'd be happy to," I said. (Church workers just love it when their people volunteer them for stuff!)

"There's just one thing." She paused briefly, and then continued. "I need you to know that I'm a Buddhist. Sheila was a Christian and would want a Christian funeral. But after you and your pastor are done with the Christian part, I'm going to bring in some Buddhist monks to do the Buddhist part. Are you okay with that?"

I closed my eyes, and I felt my heart sink even lower than it already was. I wasn't sure if I was okay with that. I believe with all my heart that Jesus is **"the way and the truth and the life"** (John 14:6), and I wasn't sure I wanted to be a part of a Buddhist funeral. After all, if we did participate in it, what kind of message would it be sending to everyone?

After a long pause, I respectfully said, "I think I'm going to need to talk with my pastor first, before I commit us to that. Can I call you back after I talk to him?"

She understood, and we agreed to talk again soon. I hung up the phone and just wept. I had experienced death before – even the death of a peer – but this felt so different. This felt like a spiritual battle, and I wasn't sure I was ready for it. So, I immediately called my pastor. Pastor Wayne Koenig had helped my family through some difficult transitions my senior year of high school, and he officiated at our wedding years later. I had worked for him a few summers running Vacation Bible School and some youth programs at the church. He is an incredible man and I felt that I knew him well – and yet I honestly had no idea how he would react to this request.

I explained the whole story to Pastor Wayne and asked for his advice. Without hesitation he responded, "Of course we're going to do it! We're going to give them Jesus! It doesn't matter what they do after us!"

I felt my spirits starting to rise again, as Pastor Wayne's words rang in my ears. *We're going to give them Jesus!* I called Sheila's mom back right away and told her that we would both be happy to serve at the funeral. She thanked me profusely, and on that afternoon I started to prepare my very first eulogy.

I will never forget what Sheila looked like in that casket. All of the other open casket funerals I had been to were older people who looked like they were resting peacefully. In contrast, Sheila looked like she could sit up at any moment – but at the same time she looked cold and pale. She looked normal and lifeless at the same time. I don't really remember the words I spoke in my eulogy that day. I know I also played the guitar for a worship song – but I can't recall the name of the song. But I certainly remember that Pastor Wayne gave them Jesus! I was so proud of him and thankful for him. It was a beautiful and respectful funeral, filled with hope in Jesus!

As we were gathering our things afterward, the Buddhist monks started to arrive at the funeral home. Just as I was about to leave, Sheila's mom pulled me aside and thanked me for organizing the Christian funeral. I told her how honored I was to be a part of it. Then she said something that thrilled me and inspired me. "Jacob," she said, "Sheila was always worried about my relationship with God. I think I should check out your church sometime."

I am so happy that we did the funeral. I know that many Christians would not have done this, wanting to avoid any association with other religions. But we did it. And because we did, Sheila's mom had an encounter with Jesus.

Looking back, I now realize the irony of my initial reaction. I had worried what kind of message our participation in a Buddhist funeral would send to people – and in doing so, I had completely missed the bigger picture. The message we shared that day was one of hope. It was the message that Sheila loved Jesus and believed in Him as her Lord and Savior. It was the realization that Jesus loved Sheila so much that He gave His life for her, so that she could spend eternity with Him – and through that same sacrificial love, all who believe in Him will never die but have eternal life (cf. John 3:16). There could be no greater comfort than these words. And *that* was the message we "sent" people by being there that day!

· · · · ·

Throughout the Scriptures, we see Jesus meeting with people wherever they happen to be. He never once invites someone to the temple. He doesn't sit around in the temple waiting for the lost to show up. Instead, He goes to *them*. He is out in the streets and villages where He will encounter those who need to know Him. Even His enemies acknowledge this when they say, **"This man welcomes sinners and eats with them."** (Luke 15:2) It's amazing to think that Jesus associated with sinners, and yet He Himself never sinned. But we have a similar call. To live life as a missionary, we have be out there where we can reach the people who need us – and as we do so, we rely on God to keep our faith strong regardless of any negative influences we might encounter. God calls us to get out of our comfort zone! It might feel unnatural at first, but we do it so unbelievers will hear of the grace and truth of Jesus!

Questions for Reflection and Discussion

1. When have you found opportunities to "give them Jesus?" Were you nervous? Hesitant? Excited? Share your experiences.

2. Do you find yourself "waiting in the temple" for the lost to show up? Or are you out there living a missional life among them?

3. What would you currently define as your missional "comfort zone?" Write down three things that fall inside your comfort zone, and another three that are just beyond it. Would you be willing to reach out and try those three new things?

Top Ten Ways
to Ruin a Mission Trip

#8

Treat the Trip As a Vacation

On just about every mission trip I have been on, there is always that person who's clearly there for "the wrong reasons." Being there for the wrong reasons is actually something that excites me as a leader, and I specifically pray that God would open their eyes and heart and show them the right reason for being there. Those who come along in search of a traditional vacation are apt to be disappointed, as well as letting down other team members who are counting on their help and participation when there's work to be done. Vacationers are usually thinking selfishly – *What can I get out of the trip?* – rather than approaching the trip with a servant's heart and hands. While vacationing and Sabbath Day rests are important, they are not why we go on mission trips. To truly be on mission, we put other's needs ahead of our own as we focus on how others can be served.

That being said, I think it's important to understand the full range of short-term mission trips. The spectrum runs all the way from "voluntourism" to sociocultural immersion. Voluntourism is a trip where one works hard during the day, but sleeps in a nice hotel and spends some time exploring the country as a tourist would. Make no mistake – voluntourists are still selflessly volunteering their time and energy to help others. On the other end of the spectrum, sociocultural immersion means that you live as the local people in a specific context live. If the people live in grass huts – you live in a grass hut. If the people eat rice and beans for every meal – guess what you eat?

Both of these models, and everything in between, can be an effective means of doing mission work. But not everyone will be comfortable with every style. As much as I think it would be fun to live in a hut, my wife Christy is not that kind of missionary. While she has a huge heart for missions, she's more of a teach-English-and-sleep-in-a-comfortable-bed type as opposed to a sleep-on-the-ground-and-eat-bugs type. The key to a successful mission trip is viewing the entire trip as a mechanism to serve others, not yourself. So, although you may have to take vacation time to go on a mission trip, don't treat it like a vacation!

Finally, it's interesting to note that the meaning of "vacation" depends on the culture. While on a trip to the small city of Guarai, Brazil, we tried to translate the English word "camping" into Spanish for our new friends. After failing miserably for several minutes, we called over the translator and asked for some help. He lovingly told us that the word "camping" just doesn't translate easily into this culture. Their daily living is similar to our "camping." This is why it was nearly impossible to explain camping as a vacation of choice!

#7

Don't Keep in Touch

Thanks to today's technology, we have the incredible ability to communicate with other people like never before. I frequently remind my students that back when I was doing my internship in Hawaii, my (then) fiancée Christy was in California. We could only talk a few times a week because it cost ten cents a minute – and those minutes had a tendency to add up fast! But now, my student in Hong Kong can talk to her boyfriend in Austin, Texas every day for free with video chat on Skype^{TM}. They get to talk *and see* each other on a daily basis! I am very jealous that Christy and I didn't have this capability back in our day!

Nowadays we have so many convenient, inexpensive, and instantaneous options for staying in touch with people – Facebook$^{®}$, Myspace, e-mail, Skype, cell phones, etc. These are valuable tools for turning short-term missions into long-term missions. And this needs to be our goal. Life is a journey. God's in the business of long-term (eternal) relationships! If you want to ruin your mission trip, pop into someone's journey only once and never try to connect with them again!

I've been leading mission teams to the White Mountain Apache Reservation since 2001. During some years, we went as many as four times. In other years, we were only able to get out there once. But we keep returning! After we had been coming to the reservation for about five years, we became known as "The Team from California That Always Comes Back." This is a huge compliment! By the grace of God, we had turned a short-term mission trip into a long-term mission trip! We watched kids grow up. We said good-bye to some of the elderly. We have become a regular part of their lives, even though we are not official residents of the reservation. In 2009, when our family moved from Southern California to Austin, I continued to lead Apache mission trips, and a funny thing happened. The Texas students I brought with me were also called members of The Team from California That Always Comes Back! Now, let me explain that nothing is worse for a Texan than to be called a Californian! But they handled the compliment graciously!

If you do *not* want to ruin your mission – make sure you keep in touch! Keep building relationships. Relationships take a long time to develop, but if you faithfully invest the time and prayer, who knows what rewards God will reap?! Every relationship you develop could have eternal significance. As you look ahead to tomorrow and think about how many different people you will connect with during the course of your day – even in small ways – this idea should inspire you. The opportunities are endless! You wrote it in the yearbooks you signed in high school… Now live it – *Keep in touch!*

Before I close this topic, I want to include a quick safety reminder. You can generally feel good about giving out your Facebook name, e-mail, and possibly even phone number. (I recommend they be given out in this order.) However, especially when serving in an international context, do not give out your home address, except in rare circumstances. I've heard horror stories of people showing up at a missionary's front door after running away from their home country under dangerous conditions. So remember – keep in touch, but use careful judgment and wisdom about the information you share.

Personal Mission Perspective

Our First Mission Trip
by Maile and Leilani Youmans

I am Leilani Youmans, age 8.

And I am Maile Youmans, age 9.

After years of hearing all of our dad's stories about his mission trips all over the world, he has finally taken us on our first mission trip! We got to go to Florida during spring break of 2013. It started off with helping Connie. Connie is a very nice lady. She helps people who can't afford much. She helps people who pick strawberries and blueberries. They travel all over the country to find work, and they do not have homes. To help Connie, we put food into paper bags and took them to the workers with toys and books for their kids. It was great to see them so happy to get some food, and the kids were so cute! Then we raked leaves in the yard for them. After we helped Connie, she took us to her friend's blueberry farm. We both tried a blueberry. They were not ripe yet. They were very sour. At the blueberry farm, we saw the place where they work. They had boxes and boxes of blueberries. Picking blueberries looks like very hard work!

Next we went to the Plant City food bank. We put food into boxes. We packed more than 200 boxes! The boxes are for kids that need food over spring break. We were told to give families: (list) 1 kid = 1 bag; 2 kids = 2 bags; 3 kids = 3 bags; 4 kids = 4 bags; 5 kids = 5 bags! What happens when 6 kids come?! The list didn't say! On Saturday, we went back to the food bank and passed out all the bags we could. Some bags were for the kids, and some were for the whole family! It felt so good to help people that needed help. People kept telling us that they were so impressed that little kids like us could help so much! It was an awesome trip!

We hope to go on lots more mission trips with our dad! We want him to take us to China! Taiwan! Australia! Japan! France! And a bunch of other places! We can't wait to go to all of them and tell people about Jesus!

. . . . .

Maile and Leilani have Hawaiian names, but were born in California and now live in Austin, TX... where very few people can pronounce their names correctly. Maile means "special blessing" and all who know her agree that it is a perfect name for her! Leilani means "heavenly flower" and that describes her very accurately as well. While currently serving as full-time students, they do have a pet-sitting and plant-watering business on the side. Leilani is studying to be an astronaut and Maile is studying to be a chef.

Personal Mission Perspective

Why We Go
by Cary Hoff

One of the most common questions I'm asked when it comes to mission trips is, "Why do you go?" I've heard this from many different people, some outside the Church, and even some from inside the Church. And my answer every time is, "I go on mission trips and live missionally because my God is on a mission." We are told in John 17:18 that Christ Jesus was sent into the world with a mission, and He is also sending us into the world as part of that same mission. But this mission began long before us, and even long before Jesus walked this earth.

Our God, Yahweh, has been on this mission ever since humanity – His creation – fell into sin (Genesis 3). God's mission is to redeem His people and reunite them back to Him. Through the pages of Scripture, we are shown that God has been on a mission for us. And He even shows us how to join in His mission for others. Our God was visibly present with His people as they traveled through the desert to the Promised Land. And despite the Israelites' tendency to blatantly run away, God remained in the trenches with His people.

Our God was sacrificial when He sent His one and only Son to take our place on the cross. We are told in John 15:13 – **"Greater love has no one than this: to lay down one's life for one's friends."** Christ was (and is) our ultimate sacrifice that has reunited us back to God our Father in heaven. But our story did not end there, because three days later Jesus rose from the dead – defeating sin, death, and the devil on our behalf. And our story continues as God's Holy Spirit is sent to believers to empower and equip us so that we too may help others know of God's extravagant love for us through Jesus, His Son.

So once again, I go on missions and live missionally because Jesus has done so much for us all. God does not need us to complete His mission, yet He chooses to use us. The only appropriate response is, **"Here am I. Send me!"** (Isaiah 6:8)

Yet, it's so easy for us to get caught up in the mind-set that being missional is about our eloquent speech and ministry skills. In Matthew 10:19-20, we are reminded that it's not about our own words or abilities, but rather it's about God our Father speaking and working through us. Once again, God *chooses* to work through us rather than *needing* to work through us. Another stumbling block I've seen in myself and others is a "comparison game" of where we go for mission. Yes, we know that we can be on mission in our own back yards, but we also desire to be the one who has traveled the farthest or to the most remote and exotic places for Jesus' sake.

When it comes to mission, it's not where we go, but Who we share. I had the amazing blessing and privilege of preaching atop Pottinger Peak in Hong Kong to a varied group of high school Christians and other travelers at the lookout. I shared with them God's everlasting love found in Romans 8 and how nothing, including the vast Pacific Ocean, could separate us from Him (verses 38-39). But the face in the crowd that I will never forget was that of the Buddhist monk who emerged from the woods to hear the message God spoke through my translator and me that day. Right here in my apartment complex I have a friend named Dave who doesn't know of Jesus' love for him, and wants very little to do with the Church of today. It has been my mission to share that same message of God's everlasting love with Dave, just as it was shared with another soul 8,000 miles away on that lookout. Again, it's not where we go, but Who we share.

And finally, as much as missions are about sharing with others God's everlasting love through Jesus Christ, never underestimate the fact that God can work just as much *in* you as He can *through* you. God has taught me, showed me, grown me, and developed me so much in all of my missional experiences. It is my prayer that you will take that leap of faith and join Jesus in His mission to reunite us all back to our Father in Heaven!

· · · · ·

Cary Hoff is a recent graduate from Concordia University Texas and is completing his Director of Christian Education internship at Hope Lutheran Church in Plant City, FL. He enjoys outdoor activities and is always ready for an adventure! Cary's passion for missional living continues to lead him to serve all over the world. His many experiences in domestic and foreign missions have helped him to find true joy by being the hands and feet of Christ.

Samaria

Introduction to Samaria

In the New Testament, it seems like the only people worse than Gentiles are Samaritans! The Jews viewed them as "half-breeds," as their ancestors were both Assyrian and Hebrew. Jews did not associate with Samaritans. But surprise, surprise – Jesus changed everything! He not only talked to Samaritans, but even to Samaritan women (John 4:1-26)! He healed Samaritans (Luke 17:11-19)! He even made a Samaritan the good guy in one of His parables (Luke 10:25-37)! Geographically, Samaria is between Galilee, where Jesus was raised and where many of His disciples were from, and Judea, where He did much of His ministry.

Metaphorically, Samaria represents people who are in many ways not like us. The differences may be ethnic, economic, or lifestyle. "Samaritans" generally would not feel comfortable in our church. People tend to go to worship with others similar to them. But Jesus has called us to be His witnesses in Samaria as well. If we only witness to people we are comfortable with, we are not being responsive to the complete message of Jesus! Samaria could be one of your greatest challenges yet!

A Note about the Apache Mission Stories

In the Samaria section, you are going to read several stories about our adventures on the White Mountain Apache Reservation in Arizona. There are stories of other "Samarias" as well, but I think this particular place may need a little more explanation before you dive into this section. My first trip to Apache was in 2001, and since that time I have visited the tribe from one to four times a year, every single year. There has not been a time interval of more than twelve months since that very first Apache trip the fall of 2001.

In my life, this tribe has been an incredible, life-changing "Samaria" experience. I have spent more nights sleeping on the Apache land than anywhere except my own home. The reservation has changed the lives of the hundreds of students I have led there over the years. This place is one of the things my brother Nathan credits with saving his life. Apache has motivated me and inspired my missional thinking in ways I am still processing. I have a very special bond with this place.

The history of Native Americans, and the Apache in particular, is not a pleasant one. I believe most of you know the basics. The more I learn, the more it angers me. One of my favorite shirts has a group of Apache Warriors on it and the caption says, "Apache Homeland Security – Fighting Terrorists since 1492." The word "apache" in the Apache language actually means "enemy." For 500 years, their story has been one of brutality, broken promises, and oppression.

Visiting the reservation has often not been easy. We have had to take several students to the hospital for a variety of ailments. Every trip, someone ends up with pretty serious flu-like symptoms, and on one trip, 16 of the 21 participants got violently ill. On our first few trips, kids would throw rocks at us and tell us to "Go home!" The kids would steal anything that wasn't bolted down. We've lost hundreds of dollars to theft. We've had windows on our vehicles smashed. We've had people bang on the doors of the building we're staying in at 4 A.M. – just to freak us out. We've stayed in rooms with no heat in the freezing dead of winter, and no air circulation in the scorching heat of summer. We have been told "White men cannot be trusted." We have been marginalized due to the color of our skin. But we have also made lifelong friends, and we have seen people come to Jesus in the process.

Through it all, we have tried to continue to love like Jesus would love. We have tried to focus on our similarities as human beings – not on our differences. We have tried to show those who still worship the sun the power in worshiping the One who created the sun. And while we have failed many, many times, we have also seen God work in miraculous ways many, many times!

I truly believe this book would not have been possible without the White Mountain Apache relationships God has blessed us with. I have had a dream since 2004 that we would be able to place a full-time missionary with the tribe. There were many people over the years who I thought would be that person. Matt Wingert spent a summer there by himself. Several others spent weeks here and there. And by the grace of God, in August 2012 that dream became a reality as Lydia Humphries started her yearlong internship on the White Mountain Apache Reservation! And as she finished that up, she told me in April of 2013 that she will continue to be serving in Apache for the foreseeable future! Our journeys to the reservation are a reminder that we need to be patient and just let God work! Everything will work out in His good and perfect time!

Where's Warren?

I grew up at the height of the *Where's Waldo?* book craze –
but I never got it. I never understood why those books were
so popular, and I certainly didn't have the patience for them. I
always figured if Waldo wanted to be found, he wouldn't
hide in a stupid book wearing a stupid sweater that looked
like everything else in the book.

On a mission trip to the Apache reservation, we found
Warren. The crazy thing about finding Warren is that we
weren't really looking for him – yet we found him. We met
Warren in the parking lot of a grocery store. He asked if we
would give him a ride home, and of course we said, "Sure,
we'd be happy to."

In spite of my desire to avoid stereotypes, you need to know
that Warren was obviously and unapologetically drunk, and
in an exceptionally foul mood. But we took him home
anyway. He needed someone to show him some kindness. All
the way to his house, he told us how much he hated God. He
told us about how his girlfriend was in jail for "a crime she
didn't commit." He told us several times how stupid we were
for believing in a God that you can't see, touch, or feel.
Warren didn't believe in the native religion either, but he
made it clear that worshiping the rock, sun, and tree made
more sense than worshiping Jesus. In the short twenty minute
drive to his house, he threw literally hundreds of spiritual

questions at us and then made fun of us for not answering all of them right away.

I told Warren that I would love to try to answer all of his questions, and that we would be around town for the rest of the week. We invited him to come by the church anytime, and we told him we'd be happy to sit down and go through all of his questions. He sneered at us defiantly and said, "No, *you* come to *my* house and answer my questions!"

"I would love to," I replied. "I'll come back tomorrow."

At that moment, it was as if he instantly sobered up. He looked me dead in the eyes, as if looking into my soul, and said, "You'd better come! Everyone says they will come but nobody ever comes!"

"Warren," I calmly reassured him, trying to look directly into his soul as well, "I *promise* you I will come over tomorrow."

We dropped him off at his home. We also met his sister Olivia and three-year-old niece Sunshine, who were worried sick about him. As we left, we told them that we would be praying for them and that we looked forward to seeing them tomorrow.

So the next morning, a few of us climbed into the rental van with a few toys for Sunshine, and a few books for Warren to give to his girlfriend in jail. We got to his house, knocked on the door, and sure enough, Warren answered. He took one look at us and frowned. "Who are *you*?!" he barked at us.

"We're the people who picked you up in the grocery store parking lot last night and brought you home," I said.

"I don't remember that," Warren snapped. "I was drunk last night." (We didn't really need a reminder!)

"That's okay," I said. "Well, we brought some toys for your niece Sunshine, and here are some books for your girlfriend to read. We just want you to know that we're praying for you, and that we will be up at the church for the rest of the week, if you want to talk to someone."

Warren took the toys and books, and slammed the door without saying another word. So we got into the van and went back to the church.

I don't really know why, but it just felt like we had to go back. So the next day we drove to Warren's house again. We brought more toys and books with us. We had been praying that God would do something, but weren't really sure what that "something" would be. We knocked on the door and Warren's sister, Olivia, answered.

"Warren's not here," she immediately informed us. "He's up in town. Our brother Jimmy's in the hospital."

"Oh, no! We're so sorry to hear that," I said. "We'll be praying for him!"

"Thank you," she replied, very politely and quickly.

"Here are more books for Warren's girlfriend and more toys for Sunshine," I said, handing her the items.

"Thank you," she said again, even more quickly.

"Well, we're here until Saturday if Warren wants to talk to us. Remember, we're staying at the church up the street." We waved good-bye and headed back to the van and left.

The next day, for some reason – and really no good, logical reason! – we went back to Warren's house again. We knocked on the door and Olivia answered again.

"Hi! Is Warren here?"

"No," she said. "He won't be back all week."

"Oh, that's too bad," I said. "Well, here are more books for Warren's girlfriend and more toys for Sunshine. How's your brother Jimmy doing?"

"Fine," she replied.

Just then we noticed another little girl walking through the house. "Ohhhhhh… who's this?" I asked curiously. I had thought we'd already met the whole family.

"That's Warren's two-year-old daughter," she said. "Her mom's the one in jail."

"I didn't know Warren had a daughter. Can we bring her some toys too? We can be back in five minutes!"

"Sure," she shrugged. And off we went.

Five minutes later, armed with more toys, a blanket, and some other goodies suitable for a two-year-old, we knocked on the door yet again. But this time, Warren himself opened the door. Our chins hit the ground.

"Hey guys, come on in," he said, more polite than he had ever been before.

We didn't really know what to think, or what to say or do, but we went inside his home for the very first time. Two teenage girls from the mission team were with me, and they gave the toys to the little girls and played with them for about half an hour while Warren poured out his heart to me. He admitted that he had lied to me; he *did* remember us and he was home each of the times we had visited – hiding in the back. He apologized for the way he had treated us. I happily let him do all the talking, because I could see that Warren needed someone to listen and care about everything he was going through. He talked about how much he had screwed up his life, and how much he wanted to put it back together. He told me he had not had a drink since we gave him a ride. He explained that in the past few days he had applied for a loan to get a truck, and that he had lined up a job to start the next week. He said he had not been to church in a very long time, but he knew that Jesus was the only one who could get his life back together, and he wanted to worship with us on Sunday.

Perhaps the best part of the conversation was that I really didn't have to say anything – God did all the work! And God was speaking through Warren himself, showing him the way back to a right relationship with Him. God found Warren, and He used more than patience. He used relentless love. He used tangible things (books, toys, blankets) that people need, not just a "Jesus loves you" slogan.

Looking back, I think the most important thing we learned from our experience is that if we had just sat in the church waiting for Warren to come to us, we never would have "found" him. It's another reminder that the church is not a building – it's the *people*. The church is about helping those in need and continuing to love them in the name of Christ even when they don't want to be loved – and even when they don't seem so lovable.

. . . . .

Where is the church? That's actually a better question than *Where's Warren?* The church *is* everywhere when we live life as a mission trip. Jesus talks about how where two or more are gathered in His name, He is there as well. You can read this in context in Matthew 18:20. We shouldn't view the church as a building with four walls, but as the people of God, wherever they happen to be. With that mind-set, we realize that the church has no geographical restrictions. It is truly *everywhere*: at work, at home, at school, at the baseball field, at the supermarket, around the community, and in the neighborhood.

Jesus showed Warren His love through a persistence that didn't always make sense to those of us who were called to persist. But now that we've found Warren, we want to find all the Warrens of the world! My hope and prayer is that the church is wherever God is… *everywhere!*

Six months later, we were able to return to the Apache reservation, and as soon as we got into the village we went over to Warren's house. I knocked on the door, and an older Apache woman answered whom I had never met. "May I help you?" she asked, a little concerned to see a flock of white faces at her door.

"Yes," I said, smiling kindly at her, "I'm a friend of Warren's. I met him last summer. Is he around, by any chance?"

Her mouth dropped open, and she stared at me for a moment. Then she exclaimed, *"You're that guy!"*

Not sure what she meant (I've been "that guy" many times, and it's usually not a good thing), I explained to her who I was, and about the mission work we were doing with the church up the road. She just started crying and saying over and over, "Thank you! Thank you!"

It turns out that the woman I was talking with was Warren's mother. After our visit last summer, Warren got baptized. Warren married his girlfriend when she got out of jail, and she was baptized too. Warren started looking for work and found a roofing job in Florida. He then moved there with his family to start anew. God truly found Warren and gave him a whole new life – in this life and in the next!

Questions for Reflection and Discussion

1. Have you ever had someone avoid you or ridicule you for your faith? What was that experience like?

2. In what ways have you shown love to someone who didn't want to be loved at first? Did you see a change in them?

3. Why is it so important that we continue to demonstrate love toward people, even if they reject us? What are we able to demonstrate to them through a persistent love?

Cleaning the Park

There are several decently equipped playgrounds on the Apache Reservation, yet whenever we would drive by, I never saw kids playing on them. On one trip, our team took a closer look and realized why no one was playing there. Broken glass from whiskey and beer bottles was scattered everywhere. Several pieces of equipment were broken. In general, the place was filthy. To us, it looked like an opportunity for a good team project!

But this time, instead of simply doing all of the work ourselves, we thought it would be more beneficial to encourage the children of the community to work with us. This would show them that the playground was available to them, as well as help them establish pride in their community and teach community service. Sounded like a win-win situation! As an added incentive, we went to the grocery store to buy supplies for lunch, so we would all eat, work, and play together. What could go wrong?

When we arrived at the park, we sent about half of our group to wander through the community to recruit children to help us. Others started making sandwiches for lunch, and the rest began the hard work of fixing and cleaning up the park. It wasn't long before we had a virtual army of little children gathered. We all prayed together, asking God to bless the food and our efforts, and then we attacked the lunch. While everyone was eating, we explained what we would be doing that afternoon. Not surprisingly, the kids seemed much more excited about eating and playing than cleaning and fixing.

At one point, I got a little frustrated that our plan was not working perfectly. So, I grabbed a few extra trash bags and walked over to three little girls sitting near the slide. Having two little girls of my own back home, I figured I was the one who had the best shot at connecting with them. I started with some fun and playful small talk. They happily smiled and laughed along with me. Then I grew very serious and told them I really needed their help – and that the important job I had for them was something only *they* could do. "Will you help me pick up trash and clean up this park for you?" I asked, as I reached out my arms to hand them garbage bags. Still smiling, they didn't even need to think about it for a millisecond.

"No," they said. And off they went – back to playing on the recently fixed slide.

I was a little discouraged, but figured I could drown my sorrows in all the work that needed to be done. But an interesting thing happened. No more than five minutes later, I noticed that those very same girls were all picking up trash. They were under the direction of one of the college students who came with us on the trip. Coincidently enough, she was someone who had always thought that kids hated her!

How did she get them to help? With all of my parenting experience, education, and family ministry training, I could not inspire those little girls to work. But this college student with an aversion to kids could do it. It didn't make any sense! Later that day, I asked the student how she was able to get those girls to work with her. She was confused by the question. "I tried to get them to help me but they wouldn't," I explained. "What did you say to get them to help?"

"Nothing," she shrugged. "They just came up and asked me if they could help."

. . . . .

In Ephesians 2:10, St. Paul writes: **"For we are God's handiwork, created in Christ Jesus to do good works, which God prepared in advance for us to do."** God is preparing good works for us to do. And maybe you are the only one who can do the specific good work that God has in mind. Everyone cannot reach every person, but everyone can reach *someone*. What if God has been preparing you to witness to someone in particular? What if *you* are the best one to reach that someone? We should have the attitude of St. Paul, who writes in 1 Corinthians 9, **"I have made myself a slave to everyone, to win as many as possible"** (verse 19). The phrase **"win as many as possible"** is an important one because it's easy for us to get discouraged when our message gets rejected. It's even easier to do nothing at all and not even try, out of fear of rejection. But when we have the mind-set of winning as many as possible, we leave the "winning" in God's hands, not ours. **"For the battle is the LORD's,"** a young David reminds us when he's up against Goliath (1 Samuel 17:47). We tend to think that we have the responsibility of converting people, but our job is merely to share the love of Jesus with others. We are expected to live our lives as a faithful and bold example of that love. But only the Holy Spirit can change the human heart! We are certainly *in* the battle, but it's not *our* battle – the battle is the Lord's!

Interestingly enough, the college student who thought kids hated her – and yet became a Pied Piper of Apache children cleaning the park! – is Nicole Seals. She is now serving as a missionary in Adelaide, Australia, working with Aboriginal Australians. Before she got there, she had never even been outside of the United States, and her only mission experience was two trips to the Apache people in Arizona. She has worked with Native Americans, and now she works with Native Australians. God is using her in miraculous ways to "win as many as possible!"

Are you open to whatever God has prepared for you to do?

Questions for Reflection and Discussion

1. Are you open to whatever God has prepared for you to do? What kinds of things do you think He has in store for you?

2. What does being **"a slave to everyone"** (1 Corinthians 9:19) mean to you?

3. How does knowing that **"the battle is the LORD's"** (1 Samuel 17:47) change your fighting strategy?

Human Jungle Gym

One of the more interesting "perks" of being six feet, two inches tall and having a big goofy smile is that little kids tend to view me as a walking, talking, irresistible human jungle gym. It doesn't seem to matter where in the world I go – the moment I meet any kids, they just start climbing all over me! And while I'm sure some people would find this rather annoying, I love it! It's a gift!

I will never forget the very first mission trip I ever went on. I was a 19-year-old sophomore in college, and we went down to the Casa de Amore orphanage in Tijuana, Mexico. About 50 kids, age ten and under, lived there at the time. It was a very simple and meager place, and certainly not aesthetically attractive, but it was well named because it was truly a house of love! The orphanage was in the main city, with large buildings, congestion, and poverty all around. We went down there to do a one-day VBS-type program for the kids.

We taught Bible stories, sang silly songs, and did lots and lots of playing. To say they had minimal facilities would be an understatement. The main play area also happened to be an old, beat-up, asphalt parking lot. There was no playground or jungle gym in sight. Fortunately, our team brought *me* along – the *human* jungle gym! The moment I stepped on the property, I instantly had 20 kids on top of me. After playing with them for several minutes, I had a kid grab my left forearm and not let go. A few seconds later, another kid grabbed my right arm and also refused to let go. At that moment I decided to give them the ride of their life. So I picked up my arms and, with them holding on and cheering, I spun around about 20 times – much to their delight! They held on very tightly as their legs flew out from under them. For a few seconds they were airborne and felt the freedom of flight.

As I carefully brought them in for a landing, I noticed that all 50 orphans were now in line for the ride! So I spun and I spun. I spun as I have never spun before! Dizziness did not stop me. Fatigue did not stop me. The sun was hot that day, and someone graciously brought me a bottle of water after an hour or so. But after a few quick sips, I kept spinning. I gave each and every one of them multiple rides on the Human Jungle Gym! No one was turned away. Everyone got their turn. It went on for hours.

But on what I believe was the one millionth spin, one of the orphans – a little five-year-old boy – did the unthinkable. He let go of my arm. I did not see it coming. I do not know if he let go by accident or on purpose – maybe he just wanted to see what would happen. The next few seconds seemed to occur in extreme slow motion as I watched this little kid's face turn from pure delight to pure terror. It was like watching a rock skip across a pond. This little boy skipped across the hard, rough pavement. Eventually, he landed. And the instant he landed, he started screaming! We ran over to help him up and found he had bitten through his bottom lip. There was now a big red spot on the black asphalt.

We knew we had to get him help. This was a bigger injury than the first aid kit could handle. But we were in a foreign country and didn't know where to go or what to do. They don't have doctors there like they do in the United States. They have what they call "El Doctors" – which means they spoke Spanish and we didn't! Fortunately, the workers in the orphanage referred us to a medical clinic a few blocks away. Several members of our group – the ones who had the best broken Spanish – took him to the clinic. They were gone for several hours, and the rest of us were waiting and praying for him the entire time! When their car pulled into the orphanage parking lot, we all cheered! The little boy jumped out of the car first and proudly showed off the 15 stitches that now resided on his lower lip. He even came over and hugged me! He was as good as new! I apologized to him over and over. He just shrugged and showed off his stitches to all the rest of the kids.

· · · · ·

Do you ever feel like the world is spinning you around and around? Maybe you blame others. Maybe you blame yourself. Maybe you blame chance and coincidence. Maybe you even blame God sometimes. That's tempting to do, because maybe – like Jonah – you find your life seemingly going belly-up, and you wonder if it's because God has it in for you. Jonah's story has always been one of my favorites. Some say it's just a parable or a myth, but I think it's a real story. In fact, Jesus Himself referenced it (Matthew 12:38-41) – so to me that's further proof that it's true!

Do you know the best part of Jonah's story? It's in Jonah 2:10 – **"it (the big fish) vomited Jonah onto dry land."** Back in Sunday School, I always had the image of the fish gently opening its mouth and Jonah simply walking out onto dry land. Nope – he was vomited. Puked. Upchucked. (I could go on for days… I have a background in youth ministry!)

But let's back up a little bit. When you read chapter 2 of Jonah, pay close attention, because it's a full prayer, written by Jonah from the belly of the fish. That's a pretty intense prayer! He had directly disobeyed God (never a good idea!) by trying to run away from a job that God had given him to carry out. He hopped aboard a ship, hoping to sail far away from his responsibilities, but a raging storm almost capsized the boat. Jonah knew he was the guilty party, so he asked the crew to toss him overboard to calm the waves and save the ship. At that point, as he sank into the depths of the sea, Jonah had to be thinking that he was going to die. He had disobeyed God, and he knew (as we do!) that **"the wages of sin is death"** (Romans 6:23). But God wasn't done with Jonah yet. Enter the big fish, center stage. Seems like God finally got Jonah's undivided attention!

Like Jonah, we all encounter storms. The world spins us around and around, and then lets us go – skipping and bruising us along the way. But here's the fascinating thing. While Jonah prayed *Save me from the storm* and then *Save me from the fish*, little did he realize that God sent those things to save him from something worse! Tragedy is actually God's opportunity!

By the way – even after the accident, the kids at the orphanage still wanted to take a spin on the Human Jungle Gym! They were not afraid to get back on the ride. Of course, I was afraid to spin them! But they were not afraid to ride, even though they saw one of their friends get very hurt. They knew the ride was still fun, and they couldn't wait to do it again. Likewise, the ride of life is still fun – even though you might get hurt. No matter what we go through, God will be there to pick us up, stitch us back together, and set us back on the right path. If you don't get a few bumps and bruises through life, then it can't be a mission trip!

Questions for Reflection and Discussion

1. Have you experienced your first mission trip? Was it what you expected? Why or why not?

2. Have you prayed *Save me from the storm* or *Save me from the fish,* and later seen how God used those difficult experiences?

3. Life is filled with excitement and challenges. What bumps and bruises have you gotten along the way?

As the Church Burns

"Jake," said the familiar but weary voice on the phone, "the church has burned down." The voice belonged to Pastor Reno Johnson, a profound spiritual, political, and cultural leader on the White Mountain Apache Reservation. I have been inspired by this man in so many ways over the years – but I have never heard so much pain in his voice.

His beautiful church was gone. It had been destroyed by an arsonist's fire – most likely set by troubled teens out looking for something to do. This church was truly a mosaic of ministry, as different groups from all over the country had assisted in the building, furnishing, and decorating of it. It was the premier church in the little town of Canyon Day on the reservation, and the apple of Pastor Reno's eye. Nothing compared to the beauty of this building.

It takes a lot to leave me speechless. But this news really impacted me. I didn't know what to say, or how to respond. Anything I could think of felt inadequate and overly simplified. It's like the feeling you get when someone close to you loses a loved one, and you find yourself desperately reaching for words that sound helpful or comforting enough. As I held the phone to my ear, I closed my eyes, and so many memories of that building flashed through my mind.

This church has held a very special place in my heart. I had slept more nights on the floor of that church than any other place in the world, outside of my own bed. I had personally witnessed so many lives changed at that place – and not only the lives of the Apache people who came there to worship, but also the lives of so many of the "missionaries" that I had led on mission teams there.

The Canyon Day Family Lighthouse Bible Church building was gone.

After what seemed like an eternity, I opened my eyes and finally spoke. "Can we still come out next week for our scheduled mission trip?" I hesitantly asked Pastor Reno, unsure of the wisdom of my request.

He was quiet for a few seconds – which is a rarity for this joyful and bubbly man. "We have nothing left," he said. "There is no running water, no electricity, no restrooms, no building – nothing." I could tangibly feel his hopelessness through the phone.

"I'd still love to come out with our mission team, if you'll have us," I humbly requested, feeling a little more confident that God still wanted us to make our planned trip.

"Yes, please come," Pastor Reno responded.

Not knowing quite what to expect, we decided to shorten the length of the trip. And since there were no facilities, we took fewer students (only two carloads) and only males who were up for an unpredictable adventure. I don't think we've ever driven the trip quicker than we did that day. We made minimal stops along the way, as we all wanted to see what remained of the church, and to support our beloved friend Pastor Reno.

Pulling onto the church property, the building didn't look too bad from a distance. For a moment, we were hopeful. "Maybe we can resurrect this building!" I thought. But once we got closer, it was obvious that the building was destroyed. People had already started to pull it apart and recycle the usable timber for their own houses, and they were salvaging the smaller pieces for firewood to heat their homes. As I walked into the charred building, the reality of the situation hit me. My heart sank and my knees buckled, and I had to lean against one of the blackened walls for support. *Who could have done such a thing? Why would anyone do this? This beautiful building had always been a place of hope and peace. It was a haven for the lonely and a shelter for the lost. It was a place of acceptance and comfort and love. And now it's destroyed. What would we do now?*

We spent the next several days assisting with the cleanup and demolition of the burned-out church. Piece by piece it came apart. We separated whatever materials could be reused for some other purpose from the scraps that needed to be trashed. It was some of the most intense physical labor we have ever experienced on the reservation. But the emotional stress was even greater. The altar had been completely burned up. The cross was destroyed. It was the quietest and most respectful I ever remember seeing a group of teenagers. We all were mourning the death of this building. Combine that with the fact that we had no access to showers or bathrooms and were sleeping on a cement slab. It was truly an "adventure."

Yet, no one in our group complained – not once. Everyone just worked, and worked hard. I also noticed that everyone got along remarkably well. This was the first, and to date the only, mission trip I have been on where there was not some kind of interpersonal team member drama or frustration. We were all of one mind and one purpose – to help the Apache people recover from this tragedy.

I could not wait for the worship gathering that Sunday morning. I imagined that we would all crowd together in the little bitty old building that served as the original church building, the one that we had long since outgrown. We would come into church with our hearts heavy with discouragement, but Pastor Reno would lift us up, excite us, and motivate us. He would surely pledge to build an even bigger and better church! Pastor Reno is such a joy to listen to, and so charismatic even under normal circumstances – so I was so excited to see what vision he would cast as he preached resurrection from this tragedy.

Yes, the old church building was packed that morning. But much to my surprise, Pastor Reno did not preach of a brand new church building. In his great wisdom, he preached instead of a reminder that buildings are *not* the Church, even though we may think of it that way. The *people of God* are the Church! We may gather in buildings for order and convenience – but the true Church is the people! I should have known this would be his message, and I was rather ashamed that I hadn't realized it before then. Pastor Reno is famous for exclaiming, "Come on, Church!" whenever he feels the congregation is not responsive during one of his messages. Then, if they still don't respond as he expects, he'll say, "I'm not talking to the walls, ceiling, and floor – I'm talking to you – *the* Church! Come on, Church!" On this day, Pastor Reno gave me hope in a way that I didn't expect but certainly needed. *We* are the Church!

· · · · ·

In Matthew 16, Jesus and his disciples are having a conversation about rumors they have heard about Jesus. He asks them, **"Who do people say the Son of Man is?"** (verse 13). The responses are varied, but then Peter gives his answer: **"You are the Messiah, the Son of the living God"** (verse 16).

Jesus loves this answer! Jesus affirms Peter by saying: **"I tell you that you are Peter, and on this rock I will build my church, and the gates of Hades will not overcome it"** (verse 18). This is the first time in the Gospels that Jesus even uses the word "church," and He states that Peter's testimony – and all who put their faith in this truth – will be the foundation of the Church. Jesus is reminding us that the Church is the people! God works in and through His people to proclaim His love to a hurting world, a world that feels beaten up and burned down, a world that feels hopeless.

Speaking of hurting, beaten, burned, and hopeless, Jesus also reminds us that the Church will prevail. Even the powers of hell cannot stop the Church, because Jesus is working in and through the Church. Buildings will fall down, but the Church of Jesus will remain forever! So, what does being the Church mean to you? Have you ever really thought about it before? When your understanding of the Church is broadened, its potential becomes unlimited!

The Canyon Day Family Lighthouse Bible Church has not yet rebuilt its burned building. But by the grace of God, the congregation is going just as strong – if not stronger than ever, because the people know and understand that *they* are the Church, and neither the fires of an arsonist nor the fires of hell can overcome them!

Questions for Reflection and Discussion

1. Who do you say Jesus is? Why?

2. When you think about "the church," do you think of buildings or people? Why?

3. How have you seen God overcome tragedy?

Top Ten Ways
to Ruin a Mission Trip

#6

Keep on Schedule

Americans love their schedules. To survive in our culture, it is essential to be on time when you have appointments and commitments. Our work days are scheduled right down to the minute. We can't seem to function without our planners and calendars in front of us at all times. But not every culture is that way. While serving in Hawaii, I learned about "Hawaiian Time" – which means it starts when everyone gets there. In Alaska, I learned about "Alaskan Time" – which also means it starts when everyone gets there. In Apache, I learned about "Apache Time"... Guess what that means? When we travel to different regions and try to force our schedules on these cultures, we miss out on opportunities to connect, build relationships, and share the Gospel. We see gaps of unscheduled time and automatically assume that they are wasted, unproductive moments. But often, what we perceive as doing "nothing" is actually a very significant "something" to those in a different cultural context.

I had an intern who once led a mission team to Apache. Every single person in our group had more experience on the reservation than did the leader, but due to my youngest daughter's birth I was unable to go and sent the intern as the official team leader. As mentioned previously, Apache Time is Apache Time. They start when they start. They will tell you a time they will be somewhere, and most likely they will not be there at that time. But sometimes they are, so you always need to be ready!

Pastor Reno Johnson is our main Apache contact and has lived an incredible life worthy of his own biography, as he has led his people as chairman of the tribe, police chief, tribal council member, as well as serving as a pastor! He is a very busy man, and when he comes for a visit you stop everything you are doing and just sit and listen to him, and take in his wisdom and experience.

Well, this well-meaning intern had a schedule to follow, and he took great pride in leading the group and following his well-organized agenda. One late afternoon, Pastor Reno showed up to meet with the group. The intern thanked him for coming but told him that because it was time for them to go to dinner, they couldn't stay to talk with him. Fortunately, all of the students on the trip knew Apache Time and lovingly "mutinied." They insisted that Pastor Reno stay, and assured the intern that dinner could wait.

This could have been very damaging to our long-term relationship with the tribe. People come first; relationships come first. In fact, in any missional context, people should *always* come first! Whenever possible, schedules should be adapted in order to make time for people and to connect with them. In that particular example, inviting Pastor Reno to come along with the group to dinner might have been a way to accomplish both. I do not believe all scheduling is bad. Scheduling can be very good, and is more necessary on certain trips and in certain contexts. But, the two most important words on a mission trip are: *Be Flexible!*

#5

Remind Everyone How Important You Are

It's so easy for us to come across as prideful on a mission trip. Even without saying anything, our financial resources and western ingenuity can be interpreted as arrogance. Pride is a very effective way to ruin your mission trip. Warnings against pride are common in Scripture, especially in Proverbs. The "conquering, great white, all-knowing missionary" is an all too common approach that often does more harm than good. Even though most of us do not intend to be haughty, the fact that we might be perceived this way in cross-cultural settings is something we all need to be aware of.

There is a story I've heard from more than one person about some of the first missionaries to Africa who established a church and baptized several people. The missionaries were told by the village Elders, "We had no idea how poor we were, until you told us." The Elders were not referring to spiritual poverty. They were talking economics. These missionaries brought quite a bit of "western culture" with their Gospel message!

On almost every mission trip I've taken to a developing nation, I've had a student say to me after a day or two, "They have no idea how poor they are." I don't respond, except with a smile. Why? Because those same students always come back to me a week later and say, "They may not have much money, but they are so rich in family, community, love, and joy!" When we measure others by our own cultural standards, or focus too much on all the things that *we* have, or all that *we* know, we can miss opportunities to learn and grow as we encounter different peoples and cultures.

Being a citizen of the wealthiest country in the history of the world certainly has its disadvantages. Missionary friends serving in poorer countries say the "damned if you do, damned if you don't" reality first hits when you choose a place to live. They say if you live in the village with the people, you are labeled an idiot because you could live better but chose not to. But if you live in the manner you are accustomed to, you are viewed as a snob and not one of the people. What eventually breaks down the barrier is *love* – love that focuses on our similarities as people, and not on our differences.

I've heard so many well-meaning mission group leaders say things like, "I get more out of mission work than I give," or "Mission work is hard, but great is your reward in heaven." These things may sound nice – and I know they are well-intended – but statements like these focus on our differences and set up a "transaction" mentality. There is a "giver" and a "getter" in these statements. When serving others, it's all too easy to look for some kind of transaction. But I encourage you to always turn the praise, honor, and glory back to Jesus! It's all about Jesus. It really has nothing to do with us. We are simply the tools He has chosen to use at a particular time and place.

When I'm asked to "say a few words" to address the community during mission trips, I always keep it as short as possible and simply say, "Thank you so much. We love you. And remember, Jesus loves you even more!" I want them to simply see Jesus. We are all in this life together. God's love unites us, and I want everyone we work with to know that it's not about me or our group; it's all about Jesus!

#4

Focus on Romance

I know that when the topic of mission trip romances comes up, we like to think of the successful ones. Many of us have a friend, or a friend of a friend, who met their soul mate on a mission trip, fell in love, and now lives happily ever after. While that can certainly happen (I don't want to limit God), it's certainly the exception and not the norm. The norm is heartache, infighting, distraction, and inappropriate behavior – and I could go on and on.

At the end of the movie *Speed*, after Keanu Reeves' Jack and Sandra Bullock's Annie have escaped the out-of-control subway car and are rolling around on the ground together, they have this conversation...[2]

> **Annie**: "You're not going to get mushy on me, are you?"
>
> **Jack**: "Maybe. I might."
>
> **Annie**: "I hope not, 'cause you know, relationships that start under intense circumstances, they never last."

Was Keanu Reeves in *Speed 2*? No! Why? Because relationships that start under intense circumstances never last! There are few spiritual circumstances that are more intense than a mission trip. You are experiencing spiritual warfare in new and different ways. You are out of your comfort zone. You are experiencing a different culture. Focusing on romance will cloud your thinking and your judgment, and keep you from realizing the full potential of the mission God has blessed you with!

As dangerous as team member romances can be, let me place an even greater warning on becoming romantically involved with the local people. This can be so confusing to them – and to you! There is nothing more attractive than someone who loves Jesus and serves Him with their life, but romance is a trap that Satan has used to destroy the ministry of many, many missionaries and church workers. It is best to avoid any romantic contact and strive for a life above reproach, especially in this area. Do not be alone with anyone who is not your spouse. Always be in groups. There is safety in numbers, especially when it comes to this issue.

I also need to give a word of warning in regards to appropriate dress in different cultures. Many cultures are significantly more modest than our American culture. For example, in some cultures, women wearing shorts is offensive. Dressing this way will minimize or discredit your message. While in North Africa, I wore long pants and button-down collar shirts, and the women in our group covered their heads, in order to try to fit in and be respectful of the culture. Another thing to remember is that certain interactions that might be considered charming or harmless flirting in America could be very offensive in other cultures. It is important to learn as much as you can about a culture before you engage it! May the only love we share be the everlasting, eternal, unchanging love of Jesus!

Personal Mission Perspective

What is God Calling You to Be?
by Nicole Seals

One question that grownups like to ask youth is: "What do you want to be when you grow up?" Now, there is nothing wrong with this question; it's healthy for kids to consider their future and make goals. I, too, was asked this question throughout my early life, and while my answer may not have stayed consistent over the years, I always had a response. My answers ranged from joining the Navy to becoming a marine biologist, cosmetologist, teacher, and museum curator. A bit spastic? For sure! Every time I changed direction in life (or my major in college) I had my life planned down to the detail. For my fellow detailed-oriented planners, I'm sure you can relate. For those who may not understand, let's just say the only time I "went with the flow" was when I dug the ditch myself and poured the water. That kind of "flow" was the only type I was comfortable with. Looking back, when it came right down to it, I wanted to be happy and passionate about my choice of vocation. Nothing wrong with that... right? Yes, but through the question of what I want to be when I grow up and the plans I always made, I always left out the most critical detail of all – God.

To show you what I mean, I will take you back to the last semester of my senior year at Concordia University Texas. I had changed my major for the last time to multidisciplinary studies, with a concentration in history and English. At this point, I had decided I wanted to go on to graduate school for museum studies. I love research, reading, and sharing facts with people. It seemed like a natural transition to the next part of my life. Being the great planner that I was, I had already taken my GRE, submitted my grad school application with essay, and had my letters of recommendation sent in. As an undergraduate, I had been heavily involved with student government and served on various committees, had a good GPA, and my test scores were above the recommended average. What could go wrong? Well, as it turns out, *everything*. I will forever remember the day I opened up the e-mail I received from the university I had applied to, saying that they regretted to inform me I was not accepted into their program. I was shattered. I felt like I had failed... No, Nicole Seals did *not* fail. Maybe she hit a bump in the road, but she did not fail. Yet there it was, in a couple sentences, a life-altering message. To add salt to the wound, graduation was about a month away, so everyone was asking me, "What are you doing when you graduate?" For once in my life, I didn't have an answer to their question. So I would jokingly say, "Walk across the stage, of course!" The only thing I *did* know was that I would be going back to the Apache reservation with Dr. Youmans on a mission trip the week after graduation. I had gone on my first mission trip with him the year before, and I was hooked! Serving people and just loving them as children of God was something that felt very natural and comfortable to me, and I needed something comfortable at that point in my life.

As it turns out, there was a pastor from Australia visiting the States at the same time we were on the Rez, and he wanted to see what life was like for the Native Americans. He came out for two days and I learned more about his ministry. It turns out that he was the pastor of a Lutheran church in Adelaide, Australia that ministered to the Aboriginal community of South Australia. There were many conversations about the similarities and differences between the native people of both countries. He also spoke about the lack of leadership he had in his church, and what a struggle it was to start programs because of the dynamics of his congregation and the culture of the Aboriginals. He then made a side comment about how lucky he would be just to have *one* young person who was passionate about the Lord to come and help his church. (Since over half the people in our group were studying to be in ministry, you could understand the envy a pastor in his position would have!) After he said this, a thought entered my head – *Go to Australia.* While this thought was going through my head, I also felt it in my heart, or more like my whole chest. It was an odd sensation and I'm not even sure how to fully describe it, but I fully believe it was God speaking to me. A little while later, we had prayer partner time, and there was an odd number of students so I was paired with Dr. Youmans. We decided to take a walk on a dirt road by the church, which is where I told him about the revelation I had during the pastor's talk. He didn't give me any strange looks – just a smile, and he said, "Well, let's see what we can do, and pray about it."

Long story short, I am writing this as I sit here in my room in Adelaide, Australia. While I could go on about the details of what happened to get me to this spot in life, I'm not going to do that in order to illustrate a very important lesson. Details do not matter – and planning the details do not matter – unless you include God in them. I had the pleasure of skyping with Dr. Youmans the other day, and he made a comment about how well I am doing in a foreign country because I embrace my independence. I thought about this idea after we ended our chat, and I must say that after reflecting on it, I must respectfully disagree. I have fully embraced my *dependence*. You see, I was trying to plan and do everything independently, and we all saw how well that worked out. It is independence that takes us away from a plan already made for us. When you are considering a vocation, it is important to realize you must have full dependence on God. Even with all of my detailed planning for all my other "paths" in life, I was never fully at peace with my decisions. But here, thousands of miles away from my family, friends, and the life I spent 22 years building in central Texas, I have never been more at peace with a decision than I am right now. With dependence on Him, I fully believe that **"the peace of God, which transcends all understanding, will guard your hearts and your minds in Christ Jesus"** (Philippians 4:7). I don't know what your defining moment will be like when God calls you, or maybe He already has. I do know that our God is a God of wonders, and He never calls people the same way twice. It is something intimate between the two of you, and that is where the peace enters your life and the dependence grows and prospers.

· · · · ·

Nicole Seals is currently serving in Adelaide, Australia to complete her two-year internship to become a Director of Christian Education. Besides a passion for ministry, she is an avid American Football fan and proudly supports the Pittsburgh Steelers. Her parents live in Georgetown, Texas and she has an older sister who lives in Arlington, Texas and another older sister and brother-in-law who live in Dallas, Texas.

Ends of the Earth

Introduction to Ends of the Earth

This one is the most self-explanatory. Literally and metaphorically, Ends of the Earth is, well, the ends of the earth... It is every corner of the earth. It is every tongue and every tribe on the planet. Throughout the Scriptures, we see that God's love is for the whole world.

This one might require you to travel – plane, train, or automobile – your choice. And this one is definitely going to require you to meet people not just different from you – but *very* different from you: different languages, different cultures, different in nearly every way. But even though things will be different, you will also get to explore some of the things that are similar among the people of the world. You will learn the power of a smile and nonverbal communication – even wacky hand-motion-sign-language-communication. You will learn that family is a universal value, and can also cause the greatest pain in one's life. You will learn that just because there is a lack of financial resources does not mean there is a lack of joy. You will learn that love really is a universal language.

And just in case you get car/train/plane-induced motion sickness – I have good news for you too. God is bringing the world to you! In the larger cities in the U.S.: Los Angeles, Houston, New York, Chicago, etc., there are hundreds of different languages spoken. Even the smaller, more rural towns in North America are becoming more culturally diverse. Because of the unchurched population here in the U.S., we're the third largest mission field in the world behind China and India! In fact, I have met people from countries as

far away as Korea who are coming *here* to serve as
missionaries… in North America!

The Ends of the Earth could be at the end of your street! Let's
explore what it means to be a witness to the Ends of the
Earth.

Higher, Higher, Higher

During a visit to Hong Kong to visit Andrea, one of my missionary interns, I had the opportunity to watch her lead an opening assembly at a government subsidized school. While this school is government-funded, it is run by the Lutheran Church-Hong Kong Synod. It's a fascinating model that enables them to talk about Jesus in public schools! Every morning during this assembly, Andrea led the singing of an upbeat "Jesus song" in English, and prayed with all the students and teachers – many of whom did not know Jesus Christ as Lord and Savior. She would then make a few announcements, and send the students off to class. What an uplifting way to start the day!

I had an incredible time while in Hong Kong and had the opportunity to meet with many of the wonderful missionaries, teachers, and students at the school. They were all very kind, friendly, and thankful for my visit – as well as much too generous. Of course, there was a language barrier, but both sides were very gracious and patient during the occasional moments of confusion. During my final day in Hong Kong, the principal came to me and asked in his best English: "Dr. Youmans, would you lead us in the opening song today?"

"Of course!" I said, without even thinking about it. "I would be honored!" Little did he know how much I love to be up on stage and work a crowd – especially a crowd of kids! These kids were a very excitable bunch, and I was fired up to work with them.

I borrowed a guitar, got up on that stage, and led the whole school in a classic kid's song called, "Cast Your Burdens." First, I taught them the chorus:

> Cast your burdens unto Jesus
> For He cares for you
> Cast your burdens unto Jesus
> For He cares for you

They are simple words, but beautiful and true. The kids were really enthusiastic about singing this song. We taught them the hand motions, and they sang at the top of their lungs! Then it came time for the first two verses:

> Higher, higher
> Higher, higher, higher
> Higher, higher, higher
> Lift Jesus higher, higher
> ...
> Lower, lower
> Lower, lower, lower
> Lower, lower, lower
> Stamp Satan lower, lower
> ...

Everyone – the principal, all of the teachers, and of course all of the students – sang these verses as loudly as they could! They jumped up so high during the "higher" part, and squatted so low during the "lower" part. It was incredible! At that moment, I was feeling like the greatest missionary in the history of the world!

After I finished, I left the stage to thunderous applause. I waved to the crowd as I went on my way. The principal then got on stage and very graciously thanked me so much for coming to minister to them, and they prayed over my travel home.

Several days later, I got a phone call from Andrea in Hong Kong. She told me that the day after I left, she had planned to start off the assembly with the same song I had done – "Cast Your Burdens" – since everyone liked it so much the day before. However, right before she was about to go on stage, the principal pulled her aside and very kindly told her not to sing that song anymore. Very curious and confused, she asked why not. Well, it turns out that phonetically, "higher" sounds just like a Cantonese swear word that is essentially our "F-word." So, apparently I had 500 students – not counting faculty and staff – jumping up and down and singing at the top of their lungs:

> F-word, F-word
> F-word, F-word, F-word
> F-word, F-word, F-word
> Lift Jesus F-word, F-word

Language has power! Obviously I had no idea of the offense I was committing, and the people were too polite to tell me directly. But I learned a valuable lesson about the power of our words!

· · · · ·

Words have the power to build up and the power to destroy. There are several verses and Bible stories that connect to this idea. For example, take a look at the account of the Tower of Babel in Genesis 11:1-8. This story took place after the flood, and the people of the world all had one common language. They decided to build a tower to heaven – to be like God. In verse 6, God makes this fascinating observation: **"If as one people speaking the same language they have begun to do this, then nothing they plan to do will be impossible for them."** When we are united in language, anything is possible!

Language unites and connects, which is why it is so important for missionaries to use the proper "language" and cultural references. For example, it would make no sense to talk to a person who lives in the heat of the jungle about snow and ice – and we probably won't connect well with the person in the Arctic by using references about life on a tropical beach. We need to use language that people relate to easily and understand. This is why Jesus taught in parables. Farming, weddings, sheep, robbers, and such were everyday elements of life that the people of that time could relate to. Parables are a great form of common language. (To learn more about the use of parables and relatable language to reach people with the Gospel, you might want to read my first book, *Talking Pictures: How to Turn a Trip to the Movies into a Mission Trip* (2010; Tri-Pillar Publishing).)

The reverse of the Tower of Babel occurred at Pentecost (Acts 2:1-41). Jesus had given His disciples the Great Commission (Matthew 28:18-20) and promised the Holy Spirit would come to empower them to fulfill this commission (Acts 1:4-8) – and what did the Spirit do? The Spirit made it so everyone present heard the Gospel message in their own language. The people were amazed and said: **"Aren't all these who are speaking Galileans? Then how is it that each of us hears them in our native language?"** (Acts 2:7-8). The Great Commission may seem like an impossible task. But God has equipped us with language – and a united language makes all things possible! As followers of Jesus, the united language that we all share is God's love. Love is the one true universal language, because it transcends all barriers and differences!

I was also reminded of the power of language on a trip along the H-3 highway in Hawaii one year. I was driving a minivan full of youth across a lengthy bridge. We were singing and having a great old time, but then without warning – the back tire blew out! My instincts just kicked in and I threw the CornNuts® I had in my left hand at my copilot. I regained control of the vehicle and pulled over onto the very narrow shoulder on the side of the road. We got under the car, took the blown out tire off, and replaced in with the spare. All the while, traffic was speeding past us at 70 miles per hour – 15 over the speed limit! It was quite possibly the worst place on the island to blow a tire. But we got it fixed and soon we were back on the road. Apparently, this incident made a lasting impression on the youth who were with me that day. Two years later, when some of those students were graduating, our youth group was having a time of affirmation and several of them told me that when our tire blew on the H-3 was when they knew I was legit. "What do you mean?" I asked.

"When the tire blew out," one of the students explained, "you had no time to control yourself or even think – and yet you didn't say any swear words. I don't know *anyone* else who wouldn't have sworn in that situation!"

I had never thought about it like that before. They were paying attention to what I *didn't* say as much as to what I *did* say!

St. James says it like this in James 3:9-10 – **"With the tongue we praise our Lord and Father, and with it we curse human beings, who have been made in God's** likeness. **Out of the same mouth come praise and cursing. My brothers and sisters, this should not be."** Our words have power! The power to praise, bless, and affirm – but also the power to curse, degrade, and insult. When on a mission trip, we always try to be very careful about what words we use and don't use. Should our daily lives be any different?

Questions for Reflection and Discussion

1. How careful are you in choosing your words? Why is it always a good idea to use wisdom and care in the way we say things?

2. What do your words and actions say about you as a follower of Christ?

3. Do you have any examples of your words betraying you?

The Sniper

At the beginning of a trip from Honolulu to Los Angeles, I shuffled onto the plane and found my seat. As I was putting my stuff away in the overhead bin, I couldn't help but notice the title of the book my seatmate was reading: *The Sniper's Handbook*. Now, most of you already know that I am usually friendly and talkative with strangers, especially on airplanes. But after seeing the book this gentleman was reading, I suddenly became nervous and uncomfortable with the idea of engaging in conversation with him. With all the recent terrorism in the "friendly skies," I wasn't sure what to think of a person who was reading something like that. As I settled into my seat, I quickly pulled out a book of my own and immediately focused my attention on reading so I could avoid eye contact and small talk with him.

About an hour or so into the flight, however, it came time for the complimentary beverage and snack. And then it happened… He said something to me. "Can you hand me that?" he asked, referring to the drink and snack that the flight attendant was holding out to him.

"Of course!" I said, thinking (and perhaps hoping) this would be the end of our contact. But in a funny twist of circumstances, it turns out that he had also noticed the title of the book *I* was reading: *The Youth Minister's Survival Guide*.

"Are you in Youth Ministry?" he asked curiously.

Still unsure as to whether I wanted to get into a conversation with this man, I decided to go for it. "Yes," I said. "In fact, I serve a little church in Aiea, Hawaii. I've been there for three years now and I absolutely love it!"

There. A conversation had started, and I knew it was my turn to ask him what *he* did for a living. The door was open now, and I had to walk through it...

"Sir," I asked hesitantly – "are you... an assassin?"

He laughed. Loud and hard he laughed, for an almost uncomfortably long time. When his laughter was complete, he sighed, smiled really big, looked me right in the eyes, and said... "Yes."

He then went on to explain that he was in the military. He made it clear that he could not get into a whole lot of detail about exactly what he did. But he also shared with me that he is a Christian. How he reconciles his chosen occupation and his faith is still something I'm processing, but the statement he made next has affected my ministry as much as anything in my life. He said, "If you do your job, I won't have to do my job."

He didn't mean: you – youth minster. He meant: you – Christian; you – follower of Jesus; you – who believes that God created the world and is still actively involved in the world; you – who believes that God so loved the world that He sent His one and only Son to live the perfect life we could never live, die a brutal death we would never want to die, and then rise again under His own power to conquer sin, death, and the devil; you – who believes in the Holy Spirit, the counselor and comforter, the power of God that lives in us and works through us. If you truly believe these things, then you can't help but share it with others. And when we share the life-changing love of Jesus, people's lives will change. They will turn away from the sinful nature and pursue what is pleasing to God. So if we do our job, then there will be a lot fewer "bad guys" for my new friend to take out!

. . . . .

Maybe it helps to think of being missional as our vocation. We might not get paid to be missional – at least not in a monetary way. But it's our calling. We are called to "follow Jesus." And when we do, He promises to make us "fishers of men" (cf. Matthew 4:19). We'll still have to work for our food, clothes, shelter, etc. But our real calling, our real job, is to be fishers of men – to be missional in our jobs and lives.

There must be something special about the "fishing" concept. Jesus' disciples came from a wide variety of backgrounds, but this is the only occupation he connects back to ministry. He doesn't tell Matthew the tax collector, "I will make you a collector of men." He doesn't tell Simon the Zealot, "I will make you zealous for men." But for some reason He connects fishing to ministry.

Here are a few connections for you to think about as you strive to fish for men. First, we have to understand what Jesus meant by "fishing." Fishing in a first-century Jewish context was not done with a pole and a worm. It was done with big nets and required great teamwork. It was not an individual endeavor. This is a great reminder for us as well – when you fish for men, use a team! Connect with people who also have a passion for ministry and work together to share Jesus' love.

Second, fishing requires patience. There are many days when even the best fishermen catch nothing. Ministry requires patience. God is the one doing the work and everything will be done in His perfect timing. We may crave instant gratification, but God sees the bigger picture. Some things cannot be rushed. And while this can certainly be frustrating, we need to remember that God's in control of it all!

Finally, fishing is hard work! It's work that certainly can benefit from experience, but it's still hard work! If you are looking for an easy job, fishing is not for you! There are major preparations required. There are long days and grueling conditions. Remember all of the storms out on the sea that scared the disciples to death? It's just an average day in the life of a fisherman.

So why be "fishers of men?" Because the reward is out of this world! There is nothing like watching the Holy Spirit grab hold of someone and "reel" them in. This isn't just about life or death – it's about *eternal* life or death. What an incredibly humbling realization to think that God could use you to help someone know about Jesus and understand who He is! That's the best job in the world!

Questions for Reflection and Discussion

1. Think about your job or chosen vocation. What are some ways that you could be missional in your line of work? If you are a full-time student, where do you see opportunities at school?

2. Why do you think God chose to compare ministry to fishing?

3. How can you be a "fisher of men?"

GOAL!

I have a confession to make. I hate soccer.

I love America football, but this game the rest of the world calls "foot-ball" is just not my thing. Many "soccer haters" proclaim the low scoring as the main reason for their hatred. But as a baseball fanatic, I appreciate the beauty of a well-pitched and hard fought 1-0 game... especially when the Dodgers win! So, low scoring isn't what bothers me. Others despise soccer for the fact that a soccer game can end in a tie. But it is possible for American football games to end in a tie, and I still love that game. So the possibility of a tie doesn't clinch it for me either.

My dislike for soccer comes from my upbringing. I grew up in Cleveland, Ohio where baseball players and soccer players didn't get along. You could say we were forced to participate in turf wars. (Imagine great finger-snapping and singing bouts, just like in *West Side Story*.) We had to share the same playing fields, and accused each other of destroying the grass with the "wrong" cleats and equipment. When I was ten, we moved to Southern California. Everyone in Cleveland warned me that baseball wasn't nearly as big of a deal there and that soccer was king. So that made me want to hate soccer even more!

However, all of that being said, whenever I visit Central and South America, I always get talked into playing a game of soccer. When on mission, as much as possible I try to live by the philosophy of "when in Rome..." And soccer is their game. They love it. It's fascinating to watch kids all over the countryside playing barefoot on dirt and rock "fields" with balls made of old newspapers and tape. It really makes you wonder what they could do with cleats on grass and with a real soccer ball!

Sports are connected to culture. Watch the Olympics for even a few minutes and you'll see just how much cultural pride is a part of athletic competitions. You've probably noticed how the athletes who win at the highest levels seem to maintain their emotional composure throughout the victory and celebration, but once they are placed on the medal stand and watch their country's flag rise in the air – with their national anthem playing in the background – that's when their tears start flowing! It is very moving and inspiring. Sports are an important expression of culture!

On a recent mission trip to El Salvador, as I was trying to be culturally relevant by playing soccer, a miracle happened. The El Salvadorian masons and the day laborers from our work site were playing alongside the two groups of Americans. We picked teams, grade-school-dodgeball-style. And I was picked fourth – which caused me to laugh out loud! Once the game started, I was minding my own business, kicking the ball when it came near me but not really having any idea what I was doing, although I'm pretty sure that I kicked the ball in the proper direction – most of the time! My teammates were yelling things at me like "Mark him!" or "Run the wing!" and I would just smile and wave. In the midst of that organized chaos, the impossible happened. The ball bounced to me at about midfield. No one else was nearby. I looked left. I looked right. I closed my eyes and I just kicked the ball as hard as I possibly could. It floated through the air like an absolute lame duck. It seemed to be in the air for hours! Then, somehow – someway – the ball bounced right in front of the goalie, and as he went for it, it bounced right over his head and landed in the goal. I had scored a goal in an international soccer competition!

Now, since I had never scored a goal in a soccer game before, I wasn't exactly sure what to do. But I had accidently seen several ESPN soccer highlights in the past. So I acted accordingly. I ripped my shirt off and ran around the soccer field, waving my shirt above my head. I then proceeded to slide in the middle of the field with my hands up in the air, in all of my triumphant glory!

While I got many high-fives for my accomplishment, my goal really had nothing to do with my athletic ability, and everything to do with my athletic *availability*. I was willing to try. I was in the right place at the right time to score that goal. It was nothing that I could create, control, or manipulate. It just happened. This is missional living! This is believing and understanding that God will put you in the right place at the right time!

· · · · ·

It has been said that timing is everything. We have all experienced situations where we were in the right place at the right time. We can probably also think of plenty of times when it seemed that we were in the wrong place at the wrong time! We place a high importance on good timing and the wisdom to know when to act and when to wait. We may even wish we had the foresight and timing of the character Gandalf, who explains to Frodo in *The Lord of the Rings: The*

Fellowship of the Ring – "A wizard is never late, Frodo Baggins, nor is he early. He arrives precisely when he means to."[3]

Throughout the Scriptures, there are references to time and timing. Creation in Genesis chapters 1 and 2 is structured and ordered in perfect timing. In fact, God created time itself to glorify Him. In Genesis 1:14 God says, **"Let there be lights in the vault of the sky to separate the day from the night, and let them serve as signs to mark sacred times, and days and years."** Like all things in creation – time is good!

In Ecclesiastes chapter 3, King Solomon tells us that there is an appropriate time for every activity under heaven. We can infer that if there is a proper time, then there is also an *im*proper time. Recognizing, understanding, and knowing these "times" are crucial.

In the book of Esther, there is the possibility of a holocaust where all of the Jews in King Xerxes' kingdom would be killed. Esther is the queen, and has the potential to stop this tragedy. But attempting to stop it could cost her her own life (Esther 4:16). She is encouraged by her cousin:

> **For if you remain silent at this time, relief and deliverance for the Jews will arise from another place, but you and your father's family will perish. And who knows but that you have come to your royal position for such a time as this?** (Esther 4:14)

"For such a time as this" is a powerful idea. It means that God has you just where He wants you – even if you don't feel it or see it. Everything works out in God's perfect time. Notice also that **"if you remain silent,"** God will still work –

but then you will miss out on the joy of being part of God's plan.

Think about the timing of the life of Jesus. The Romans ruled much of the world, and also had connected the world in ways that enabled communication and the spreading of ideas. The people of God were in despair, largely based on being controlled by the Romans. Many had given up on the God of their forefathers. It was into this world that Jesus was born. To use a sports metaphor – Jesus came in at the bottom of the ninth, with two outs and two strikes! St. Paul talks about good timing in Romans 5:6 – **"You see, at just the right time, when we were still powerless, Christ died for the ungodly."** There are several important truths that we can glean from this little verse. First, we are reminded that everything is made perfect in God's timing. Sometimes we get frustrated with God because we want things to happen according to our own timetable and not His. (The story of Abraham and Sarah's long wait for a child, found in Genesis chapters 16, 18, and 21, is a good example.) Even when we don't understand the wisdom behind it, we have to trust that God always knows the right time for everything to happen.

The second point we are reminded of here is that without Jesus, we are powerless – and it was in the midst of our weak, hopeless, sinful condition that Jesus came to earth to save us. Because of Him, we are no longer powerless! Jesus promised us power, back in the first chapter of Acts (verse 8). We have been placed in the right place at the right time and have been given power. We have been given the opportunity to be His missionaries in our daily lives.

We love to focus on our abilities. And God certainly has given us abilities and spiritual gifts to glorify Him and grow His kingdom. But I want you to remember that being

missional is more about your *availability* than your ability.
It's about being open to the circumstance that presents itself.
It's about sharing Jesus – not only with your words but with
every aspect of your life. This could be the time for you to
embrace what it means to be missional. You do not even have
to go anywhere – just pray and carefully observe the world
that God has already surrounded you with. There are most
likely people in your life that God has placed there for you to
reach out to. They may be at work. They may be at school.
They may be in your neighborhood. They may be right inside
your own home. But they are there! Perhaps the time is now.
What are you waiting for? When the ball rolls to you – kick it
as hard as you can!

Questions for Reflection and Discussion

1. Do you feel like you're more often in the right place at the
    right time, or the wrong place at the wrong time? Why?

2. Why is it so difficult for us to trust in God's timetable?

3. As you strive to live a missional life, do you tend to focus
    more on your ability or your availability? Give an
    example of how God has worked through your avail-
    ability.

4. What "time" is it in your life right now? How do you
    know?

Big Buddha

The different world religions have always fascinated me – and broken my heart at the same time. Whenever I go to a mosque, temple, etc., I see people kneeling and praying and fervently searching for answers, and I'm deeply saddened by the reality of their false understanding. It does not matter how hard they pray – the false god will not answer. It is not a very politically correct thing to say that Jesus alone is the way, the truth, and the life (cf. John 14:6), but that's exactly what He said!

While on a mission trip to Hong Kong, our group went to see Big Buddha. Big Buddha is a very appropriate name for this Hong Kong landmark, as this particular statue of Buddha is absolutely huge! It's about 112 feet tall. It's their equivalent to the Statue of Liberty – a major cultural icon.

While walking around the grounds of Big Buddha, I saw thousands of people praying, crying, and burning incense and other items to Buddha. Walking around and observing all of this caused my heart to just ache. I felt like St. Paul in Acts chapter 17 as he's walking around Athens; verse 16 says, **"he was greatly distressed to see that the city was full of idols."**

I wanted to shout out, "Jesus loves you!" but I knew that would not be a very respectful thing in that culture. The "bullhorn missionary" approach has caused some people to despise Christians. So I did what I usually do in this situation – I walked around and hummed Jesus songs. I don't know why, but this particular time I kept praying, "Lord Jesus, reveal Yourself." I do not recall ever praying this prayer before. But at that time I couldn't help but dream of what it would be like if Jesus were to come down from heaven and land on Big Buddha's head. Then the whole world would *have* to believe in Him!

Jesus didn't do that – but He *did* reveal Himself. He showed up in the most humble and unlikely of places. Just as I was praying "Lord Jesus, reveal Yourself," a janitor walked by me, pushing her cart of janitorial supplies. Hanging on that cart was a cloth grocery bag used to collect garbage, and on that garbage bag, in big bright red letters, were the words: "JESUS LOVES YOU!"

Jesus showed up – not landing on the head of the giant statue, but on the bag of a janitor. Kind of like how He showed up the very first time – as a poor human baby, lying in a lowly manger in a stable in the small, insignificant town of Bethlehem. The incarnation is so incredible because it was so unexpected. The incarnation is a paradox. It's the divine God in human flesh. As St. John says to open his Gospel, **"The Word became flesh and made his dwelling among us."** (John 1:14)

. . . . .

The Kingdom of God is unexpected as well. Jesus tells a parable about day laborers in Matthew chapter 20. Some of the laborers worked a full day's work and some only worked one hour. At the end of the day, everyone was in line to get paid, and those who worked the full day noticed that those who worked only one hour got paid the exact same amount. How would you feel in that situation? The full day workers started to grumble, and one actually had the gumption to go to the boss – the landowner – and question him on it. Here's what he said: **"These who were hired last worked only one hour ... and you have made them equal to us who have borne the burden of the work and the heat of the day."** (verse 12) Notice how difficult and burdensome he made the work sound. I'm sure that at first they all were just grateful to be hired, but when they perceived unfairness the grumbling began.

The landowner (who, by the way, clearly represents God in this story!) responded:

> **I am not being unfair to you, friend. Didn't you agree to work for a denarius? Take your pay and go. I want to give the one who was hired last the same as I gave you. Don't I have the right to do what I want with my own money? Or are you envious because I am generous?** (verses 13-15)

Talk about defying expectations! To give someone who worked a full day and someone who worked only one hour the exact same amount of pay is illogical! It's a bad business model that cannot be sustained in the long term! *But* – it's the definition of grace! Grace is the ultimate unexpected reality. We do not deserve grace – yet God freely gives it. Karma is logical. Do good things, and good things will happen to you. Most world religions have a karma concept at their core. Do good, and good will happen. But God is not limited by our logic. We expect tit for tat, but God's ways are far above such worldly expectations (cf. Isaiah 55:8-9). (And it's a good thing God doesn't give us what we really deserve – we'd all be toast!) Karma is what human nature expects, but grace trumps karma every time!

The military strives to be unexpected as well. Based on talking to U.S. military leaders over the years, not to mention watching *Braveheart* way too many times, the element of surprise is what usually leads to victory. In Ephesians chapter 6, St. Paul gives us the Armor of God concept that is directly related to the spiritual warfare that is all too real and raging around us (2 Corinthians 10:3-5). So, perhaps surprise would be beneficial for us in our mission as well! If we can be surprising in how we live out our faith, maybe – by the grace of God – we can be victorious!

As you are living life as a mission trip, how can you be unexpected? How can you love people in a way they need and understand, but not in a way they expect? How can you present God's grace in a surprising way? Sometimes we can be surprising by not reacting negatively when someone is trying to "push our buttons" or being outright offensive. Perhaps we can be surprising by sticking up for the "little guy" or the unloved. Most people, especially in the American context, have a preconceived notion, oftentimes negative, of what a Christian is like. Maybe this prejudice arose from television or movie stereotypes, or perhaps because of a judgmental neighbor. Wherever it came from, if we can defy their expectations and surprise them, we just might be able to hold their attention long enough to communicate the Gospel.

Perhaps one of the greatest compliments I have ever received – and one that I actually thought might have been an insult the first few times I heard it! – is, "Jake, I have never met a Christian like you." Then they usually go on to explain how I don't judge them like other Christians they've met, and that we can find a way to be friends even though we disagree on certain things. They are amazed at how I actually live out my beliefs in my daily life and don't just *talk* about them. To sum it all up in one word – unexpected. I do not agree with the extent of these accolades – I strive and fail, like all of us – but the take-home message is that whenever we can break through people's longstanding prejudices and misconceptions, they will sit up and take notice. When we can be unexpected, by the grace of God, doors can open!

Questions for Reflection and Discussion

1. What exposure have you personally had to other world religions? Share some of your thoughts and experiences.

2. Have you ever prayed, "Lord, reveal Yourself?" If so, what happened? Is this a prayer that you might consider praying more often, after reading this devotion?

3. What things have you seen Jesus do in your life that seemed completely unexpected?

4. What are some ways that you can be an unexpected blessing in the lives of others?

Top Ten Ways
to Ruin a Mission Trip

#3

Don't Eat the Local Food

Food! You can't have a mission trip without it! (You can't have a *life* without it!) Every culture on the planet has their twist on it. There are several popular television shows, such as *Bizarre Foods with Andrew Zimmern* on the Travel Channel, that take viewers on foodie adventures through all kinds of exotic cuisine. Some of us are adventurous eaters while others of us like to stick with what we know.

In Australia, I sampled kangaroo, and it tasted much more like beef than chicken. (But the emu did taste like chicken!) When in different parts of Asia, I've tried all types of seafood, from octopus to eel. In Thailand, I indulged in deep-fried crickets and worms. They weren't as bad as I had imagined. I suppose just about anything is good when it's deep fried! And if you think about it, we have plenty of interesting regional foods right here in America. When in New Orleans, you have to try gator and snake. The bear I ate in Alaska was a tough, gamey meat – but they turned it into a nice stew. I consider myself pretty adaptable when it comes to food, an attitude which has served me well all over the world. The most uncomfortable times at the dinner table are when a dish is served to you, and you politely ask what it is –

and they respond that there isn't an English word for it. *Oh...
that sounds good! I'll have seconds of that!*

People take great pride in the food of their culture. Guests are
offered the best foods that the hosts can give. In some
cultures, to reject food when it's offered to you is a major
insult. I urge you to do some research on the food customs of
the area you're visiting so you know what to expect. And as
different as the food looks, it's good to try it – at least a little
of it! Even though we are the wealthiest country in the history
of the world, Americans for the most part stick with fairly
"boring" food. We also have a reputation for not being very
adventurous when it comes to what we will eat. So, when
you're offered something you can't pronounce or don't even
recognize – say "yes!" As your mother probably told you –
"Try it! You just might like it!"

Also know that an empty plate means different things in
different cultures. In China, an empty plate means you want
more. So the moment you empty your plate, the host will pile
more food on – even if it's something you didn't necessarily
care for and were trying to be polite about eating! In contrast,
in Japan an empty plate means you're finished and satisfied.
So, you need to completely finish your plate to make your
host happy. You are communicating with your plate. Be sure
you know what you are communicating!

Local food is one thing, but local water is a completely
different story! In many places in the world, not even the
residents drink the local water. In some places, it isn't wise
even to brush your teeth with the local water, or use ice cubes
in your drinks. I've seen people get very sick and be unable to
do anything for several days from minuscule intakes of local
water. Freezing water will not kill all of the germs in it.
Boiling water is effective, but not freezing. As a good rule of

thumb – to keep you as healthy as possible – only drink and use water from sealed bottles.

There is a great relational power in sharing a meal. Talking and eating go hand in hand. Sharing a meal is really sharing life together. Eating is one of the uniting things about the human experience. Jesus models the power of sharing meals throughout the Gospels. Think about the Last Supper, where He introduces the Sacrament of Holy Communion (Matthew 26:26-29). Think of the times He eats with so-called "sinners" (Luke 5:29-32 and 15:1-2). The Pharisees implied that He was too, simply by sharing a meal with them! Or think about after the resurrection, when eating a meal together was proof that Jesus had risen – He was not a ghost (Luke 24:36-43)! There is power in sharing a meal together!

Instead of worrying about what's in that mysterious-looking plate of food you've just been served, try to focus on the kindness of your hosts and the pride they take in their native cuisine. Sometimes you might have to close your eyes and just take a bite – but remember that bite could open whole new opportunities for community and conversation!

#2

Don't Learn the Local Language

I have a great answer to the classic question, *If you could have any "super-power," what would you choose, and why?* I always say that my super-power would be the ability to speak all of the languages of the world, so I could tell everyone about Jesus! Think about how amazing it would be to travel anywhere in the world and quickly fit in and find connections because you can speak the language!

In reality, I am horrible at learning languages. Many of you know by now that I still have great difficulty with my own English language! But every time I enter a different culture, I always try to learn a few words of the local language. Even learning just a few words can open significant doors! People in other cultures are always pleased when they see that you want to connect to their culture by trying to speak their language. And considering the fact that many people around the world want to learn some English, teaching words and phrases in each other's language is a great way to build relationships. You might feel funny, and you'll probably sound funny! At some point along the way, you will most likely be laughed at – but you're building relationships!

When we were in Santa Ana, El Salvador, my wife Christy – who has almost zero understanding of the Spanish language – was making friends with Walter, one of the local masons. Walter spoke a little bit of English, and he told Christy that he had just gotten married. Christy responded in turn that she and I were married. Everything was going great – until our friend Steve walked over to join us. Steve is single, and Christy tried to suggest, in her limited Spanish, that Walter could help Steve find an El Salvadorian wife. Instead, what Walter heard was a suggestion that he could marry Steve!

Walter's eyes got very big, and Steve and I quickly jumped in with our broken Spanglish to explain that Christy was suggesting he help Steve *find* a wife – not *become* his wife! As awkward as that moment was, it helped us build a relationship with Walter and gave us a great story to laugh about as we worked together. When Walter's wife came to visit the work site, we were the first people he introduced her to. And throughout the week, he shared more of his story with us – about how he escaped the "gang life" and was trying to make a better life for himself. We shared Jesus in a variety of ways, and left him with a Spanish Bible so he could read it in his native language. Was he ever grateful! And the whole relationship started because Christy tried to speak Spanish to him!

I have been doing short-term mission work in the White Mountain Apache Reservation of Arizona for about 12 years now. Of all the languages around the world that I have been exposed to, the Apache language is the most difficult for me to pick up. There is a good reason why the Germans could not crack the Navajo code in World War II. These languages sound different than anything I have ever heard before.

When I am asked to preach to the Apache people, I stand up before them and start by apologizing that I will not be speaking in Apache. (Their normal worship services are 80% Apache and 20% English.) Then I tell them that despite all of the years I've been coming to the reservation, I still only know three Apache words!

The first Apache word I know is *Hon-dah*, which means *welcome* – but it also happens to be the name of their casino. So that usually gets a laugh from the crowd. The second Apache word I know is "Reno Johnson," which is the name of the wonderful Apache pastor we have been working with all of these years. But the final Apache word I know is "Jesus," because Jesus is Lord of all, including the Apaches. Jesus loves the whole world! Miraculously, God still works through my lack of Apache language. In fact, Pastor Reno has told me on several occasions, "It was as if you were speaking in Apache." I love when the Holy Spirit does that kind of thing! There is nothing more humbling and gratifying than knowing the words coming out of your mouth are from God!

Language has power, and when you learn another person's language you empower them. Learning their language shows you care about them and want to know them deeper. Nothing is more powerful than hearing the good news of Jesus in your own language!

#1

Judge!

This is Number 1 for a good reason. I personally struggle the most with this one. When you get back from a mission trip, you're on a spiritual high! You have just experienced Jesus in a unique and personal way. You have seen miracles happen and lives changed. But when you get home, no one seems as excited about it as you are. They just don't understand or care that much. So our natural response is to judge them. We judge our church for lack of support of missions (*Don't they realize how important it is?*). We judge our friends and family for their lack of prayers (*They're too caught up in their own lives!*). We judge people who could have gone on the mission trip, but didn't (*Their priorities are obviously not in the right order!*). We judge everyone for not being as spiritually mature as we are. Having just come back from a mission trip, we might actually be in a position for people to listen to us. And if they do *not* listen, then the judging gets kicked up a few notches. Judging is a surefire way to ruin our mission trip!

Two days after returning from a mission trip to North Africa where we worked with the persecuted underground church, I happened to attend a staff retreat with my church. To be honest, I don't remember what topics were on the agenda, but I was dreading going on this retreat because I had just been a part of an underground church that daily risked life and limb just to share the Gospel – and I knew that sitting around talking about typical church politics stuff was going to drive me crazy!

Interestingly enough, I had been asked to lead the opening devotion for the retreat. So I chose to walk the staff through this list you've been reading: *The Top Ten Ways to Ruin a Mission Trip*. I warned them of the temptation I was feeling to judge others right then, and I explained that I would need their forgiveness if I crossed any lines. But I was compelled to try to explain to them the life-changes I had just seen and experienced. There were certainly a few times I had to be lovingly reprimanded. Once our eyes are opened out in the mission field and we see all the poverty and persecution in the world, it becomes so easy to judge those who aren't actively doing something to help the situation.

To be missional, we need to be inclusive and not exclusive. Judging others excludes them. We need to find ways to include people in our life-changing experiences and to involve them as we share what Jesus did in us and through us while on the mission trip. We need to tell the stories of our mission, but at the same time we need to use sensitivity and wisdom so that we don't over-tell or over-share. Who knows – through our experience, others might want to get involved. But not if we judge them!

One particular thing that tends to exclude people is an "inside joke." I've seen adults do this as well as teenagers. They will be in a mixed group, with some folks who were on the mission trip as well as others who weren't. A humorous or profound memory from the mission trip will come up, and those who understand will laugh and engage, while those who don't understand will wonder what it's all about and feel left out. Then they are told things like, "You had to be there." That's a judgmental statement! It's exclusive – not inclusive!

That comment divides people rather than unites them. We might not realize the harm in it, but I've seen groups torn apart because of all the "you had to be there" moments. So make sure you find ways to include those who stayed behind. Share your stories with them! And as you describe all the things you experienced, help them to imagine themselves right there with you – and maybe next time, they will be!

Personal Mission Perspective

Stop, Collaborate, and Listen
by Ken Chitwood

While serving as a volunteer in rural South Africa, I had the opportunity to sit in on sessions of the 2009 Amahoro Gathering near Johannesburg. Organized by progressive theologians from Africa and America, it was meant to facilitate reconciliation among African leaders and missionaries serving in African contexts.

Having served as an international missionary in New Zealand for two years and having gone on various short-term mission trips to Mexico, inner-city Los Angeles, Hungary, and Indonesia, I felt I had experienced much of the world and had a balanced view of culture and world Christianity. I brought this self-justified viewpoint to breakfast on the first day of the gathering.

At my table was a short, squat, African man who spoke quietly, introducing himself as Kenzo. This unadorned man unpretentiously shared that he was the president of a seminary in the Congo. Immediately I pictured the struggle of this small black man deep in the heart of darkness, teaching bush pastors in a "click" language, in the jungle, with rain dripping through the tarp serving as their roof. I thought to myself, "I'm glad he's here to learn."

Heading to the general session, Kenzo shuffled in front of me and took his seat near the front – probably so he could hear better, I thought, knowing English was his second language. Following the moving testimony of Amahoro's leader, Claude Nikondeha of Burundi, about "ubuntu," an African philosophy-theology of community that says, "a person is a person through other persons," we took a short break. Next up was a Dr. Mabiala who was going to teach on "post-colonialism and why it matters." I was excited for the challenging session ahead to be taught by a man much more learned than me. As I took my seat, I saw my new friend Kenzo up on stage. I wondered why he was up there, and thought how awkward it would be for him to be ushered off stage. But then, as the house lights dimmed and the spotlight shined on this meek man, a sudden realization swept over me... Dr. Mabiala was, and is, none other than Dr. *Kenzo* Mabiala.

For the next hour, he taught how post-colonialism calls for a reformation of theology and practice in both the African and Western Church. He expounded that for too long the conversation in Africa has been dictated by colonial forebears and American missionaries who construct stereotypes of what it means to be "African," what it means to do "mission," and how "proper theology" looks decidedly Western. He lambasted me for being part of a system that orders and educates Africans according to Western principles, and then wonders why the square peg never fits the round hole. He called for a spirit, an approach, and a strategy, to reconstruct theology from African sources of knowledge and discourse. He argued that doing so was a matter of African identity, and impressed upon me that going about missions on this continent in any other way would not be successful.

Thoroughly embarrassed by my ethnocentric assumptions about this brilliant man, I was chastened by his words as he turned to every American in the room and told us that we needed to stop talking and start listening to Africans and Asians, Latin Americans and Middle Easterners who hold the future of Christian theology and mission in their hands.

To say the least, it was a life-changing moment. My approach to missions, ministry, and theology has never been the same since.

I've learned over the years that the greatest mistake that missionaries make is coming into a context and assuming they have all the experience, knowledge, and answers for the community they are called to serve before ever listening and learning, dialoguing and discerning just what that community needs. Not only is such a stance dangerously arrogant, it is practically unhelpful and potentially catastrophic.

In my case, at a small conference, my prejudiced assumptions only brought individual embarrassment. As a posture for mission and ministry, such despotic presuppositions become destructive when they produce unsubstantiated impressions of poverty and culture, and exacerbate negative stereotypes that reinforce and reproduce power inequalities between "the West and the rest."

There is also much promise in adopting listening as our primary posture. A Pastor Luis from Tijuana, who regularly receives short-term mission teams building homes and offering Vacation Bible School (VBS), said it this way: "If [the missionaries] would simply set aside their agendas and listen to the actual needs of my people, they could come alongside us in transformative ways."[4]

When you take Christ's call to baptize, teach, and disciple the nations seriously (Matthew 28:18-20), when you truly want to **"love your neighbor as yourself"** (Mark 12:31), your primary and paramount task should be to assume the posture of listening. Just as we are to **"be still"** and know God (Psalm 46:10), we are to **"be still"** and listen to learn what God is doing through His people in this place, and how we can join in with them to do the "transformative" work that Pastor Luis mentioned, rather than showing up and immediately telling others what we are going to do for them.

On a short-term mission assignment, or heading into long-term service, missionaries must recognize that "listening to local leaders or visiting with villagers is as legitimately a part of [missions] as is building a house, performing a mime or leading a VBS."[5]

This takes a certain humility, and trust in the Spirit, to act in a way that honors other cultures and sees God at work in places beyond our borders. It reframes the missional question from *How can I get to work with what I know?* to *How is God at work already, and how can I learn to be a part of what He, and His people here, are already doing?*

In the end, it blesses us immensely as we get to hear new theological formulations and see unique, non-Western expressions of mission and ministry, which enable us to understand and appreciate our faith more fully than our myopic Western experience can ever offer.

That was my experience at a small retreat in the hills outside Johannesburg, South Africa when "Kenzo" rocked and wrecked my worldview and forever reshaped the trajectory of my life and ministry. As vulnerable as this posture may make you, and as uncomfortable and unnatural as it may be, it is my solemn prayer that listening would become your gut missional reaction and that your ears may hear and eyes may see how God is at work in the people and places you would least expect.

. . . . .

Ken Chitwood is a passionate and creative husband, religion commentator, theologian, teacher, book nerd, and endurance athlete. He lives and serves in Houston, TX where he works with two local churches launching missional communities and house churches, training leaders, and preaching. He is a freelance writer for the Houston Chronicle, Publisher's Weekly, and various other media outlets, magazines, and blogs. He likes to spend time with his wife and two dogs, read, run, and then run some more.

Personal Mission Perspective

Mission Work from Head to Heart
by Andrea Bolognini

Many people don't like spending time with middle school or high school students, and they certainly would not want to lead an international mission trip with ten of them. But I became a missionary in Hong Kong because someone was willing to lead me as a seventh grader.

My home church had an exchange program with a school in Japan. Their students visited the United States for a cultural experience, and we went to Japan with a mission focus. Because of the exchange, I was able to house and form friendships with 14 Japanese students during my formative years. One may think that this would be enough to make me want to be a missionary, but the real change happened when I went to Japan.

Prior to going to Japan, I grew up in a Christian bubble: Christian school, Christian friends, Christian *everything*! It was not until I went to Japan that I became friends with people who were my own age but did not believe in Jesus as their Savior. As I began to care more for my new friends I realized that, as it was, they were going to hell. I became emotional, and even as a seventh grader I realized that if I am not sharing my faith with people who do not believe, then they may never know. My faith became mine on that trip, instead of a faith that my parents spoon-fed me. This was amplified by that fact that my sister (who was a ninth grader on the same trip) became hospitalized and literally almost died in Japan. I was faced with the reality that life *is* short, faith at any age *does* matter, and I needed to live a life that shares that faith. My sister's illness also demonstrated that God works through hardships and can make good out of any circumstance (cf. Romans 8:28). Because my sister was sick, a chaperone and I stayed with her for an extra week in Japan. During this time, we met many nurses, doctors, and other people we would have never otherwise met or had a chance to explain why we were in Japan.

After seventh grade, my faith continued to grow and eventually led me to a life of mission work. I went to school to become a Director of Christian Education and then did a two-year internship in Hong Kong. As I arrived in Hong Kong, I was excited about everything! I had been looking forward to it since seventh grade. I could not wait to meet people and share Jesus' love with them. The first few days and weeks were spent learning who people were, what I would be doing, and eating sometimes questionable but often delicious food.

There was an evangelist who was in charge of my two years in Hong Kong. He taught me about the people's needs and how ministry was done. About a month into my internship, I was walking with him and we noticed an old woman burning an offering of incense at a street-side shrine. The woman could not hear me, so I said to him, "Seeing her worship a false god breaks my heart. I just wish everyone would know Jesus." I expected him to agree, because I knew he was dedicating his life to telling others that exact message. I was surprised when he responded with rebuke. He told me that I have no right to push my faith on someone I don't even know. He went on to say that I did not know the woman's story or respect it, but instead just wanted her to accept *my* story. I was surprised because I did not see the harm in sharing my feelings with a fellow believer and I would never have actually said that to her or been forceful when actually talking to her. However, the evangelist taught me in my first month of mission work that it is not enough to practice relational witnessing. Instead, I needed to change my heart to truly embrace it so there is never a thought of pushing my faith on someone else. I needed to build real relationships and get to know people's stories, as opposed to making a judgment of their faith and story – which I did not realize I was even doing. I need to know and respect them in order to earn *their* respect, so I can share my message. From that day, I have tried to live a life that truly accepts the people I meet for who and where they are, instead of just outwardly accepting while inwardly judging. I am called to love them and live a life that shares the love of Jesus. From there, I trust the Holy Spirit will work miracles in their hearts.

· · · · ·

Andrea Bolognini has been blessed by mission-minded parents, family, and role models who led her on an international adventure and life! After studying at Concordia University Texas, she completed her two-year Director of Christian Education internship as a missionary in Hong Kong serving with LCMS World Mission and the Lutheran Church-Hong Kong Synod. From there, she was led back to Texas and is currently serving at ACTS Church Lakeway as the Missionary to Students. She loves that her job is to invest in people and walk with them as they grow in their relationship with Jesus.

What's Next?

Class is almost over! You're so close to "graduation" and setting off to truly live life as a mission trip. But we have to ask the questions: *What's next? How will my life be different, now that I am living life as a missionary – wherever I am, and in all that I say and do?* Your family and friends may not get it. Even those in your church may or may not support and understand the new you. But we need you to be missional! Here are a few more things to think and pray about as you get ready to wrap up this course...

God Might Like it When I'm Angry

For some reason, whenever I talk, write, or even think about the state of missions in our Church and in my own personal life, I get frustrated and angry. There is so much work to be done! Six billion people do not know Jesus Christ as Lord and Savior, and without knowing Him here, they will be spending an eternity without Him! And because I was (erroneously) taught that anger is a sin, I then get angry at myself for being angry! It's a vicious cycle!

The Hulk is a fascinating "superhero." In fact, he's oftentimes the anti-superhero. As our daughters were watching the movie *The Avengers*, even they remarked, "Daddy, we thought The Hulk was supposed to be a good guy!"

Bruce Banner – The Hulk's alter ego – has an iconic line that was used in *The Incredible Hulk* TV series (1978-1982) as well as in the movie of the same title (2008) and the movie succinctly named *Hulk* (2003) – "You're making me angry. You wouldn't like me when I'm angry." He would say this to warn off the bad guys. He could not control what his anger was going to do to him and his immediate environment. This line was always uttered right before he became The Hulk – and you knew the good part was coming!

Yet in *The Avengers*, Bruce never says this line. He doesn't really talk about anger at all. That is until the final climactic fight scene, as Bruce Banner walks into battle against the enemy, Captain America yells, "Doctor Banner, I think now might be a good time for you to get angry!" Bruce replies, "That's my secret, Cap – I'm always angry!"[6] And he instantly turns into the green giant!

I often wonder if anger gets a bad rap. While many well-meaning people believe and teach that anger itself is a sin, that's not Biblical. We see Jesus Himself get angry at the temple when people had turned the **"house of prayer"** into a **"den of robbers"** (Matthew 21:13). And we know that God is certainly angered by sin. Maybe anger isn't the issue. Maybe it's how we *deal* with our anger. Notice St. Paul's words in Ephesians 4:26 – **"In your anger do not sin."** Anger isn't the sin – but how we handle our anger can lead to life-destroying sin.

There are things in this sinful world that are supposed to make you angry. The fact that so many kids go to sleep hungry every night should make you angry. The fact that slavery still exists in our world – and not just in far off corners of the world, but right here in the USA – that should make you angry. The fact that girls and young women are abused and forced into prostitution – this better make you angry! The fact that people die every day not knowing Jesus as Lord and Savior and that salvation is found in Him alone, as a missionary who wants a fuller heaven – this should make you *very* angry!

So then the question becomes: *How are you going to deal with your anger?* Will your anger motivate you to make a difference in the world? Will your anger spur you on and encourage you to live life as a mission trip?

I believe the key to dealing with one's anger is love. Sin makes God angry, and out of his great *love* He sent Jesus to redeem us of all our sins. Why did Jesus get so angry in the temple? It was because people were preventing each other from connecting with God. Love drove Him to clean up the temple. Why did Jesus get indignant (fancy way of saying angry) when the disciples were keeping the little children from Him (Matthew 19:14)? Because He loves kids and wants the whole world to come to Him!

Speaking of love and anger, notice the second part of Ephesians 4:26 – **"Do not let the sun go down while you are still angry."** No one can make you angrier than the people you love the most. This is just a fact of life. And while I have heard some contend that this verse should be taken literally – that is, do not actually go to sleep until you have resolved your anger – that is not what I believe St. Paul means.

My experience is that I tend to say very dumb things at 2 A.M. when trying to fulfill a literal understanding of this verse. And those very dumb things that I say at 2 A.M. become extremely dumb things at 4 A.M.! Perhaps St. Paul is reminding us of the importance of resolution, of closure, of dealing with our anger properly before it's "too late" – before the "sun goes down" on your loved one's life. Is there a loved one in your life toward whom you have anger that needs to be dealt with? Maybe – motivated by love and anger at the possibility of losing a loved one – now's the time to seek reconciliation.

I need to admit that The Hulk is my favorite character in *The Avengers*. When he masters his anger, he is absolutely unstoppable. By the grace of Jesus, you too will be able to do "all things" (cf. Philippians 4:13), and maybe even get to "smash" a few things along the way – like sin, ignorance, injustice, and obstacles to the Truth. Perhaps we all need a little more righteous anger to fully embrace the missional life that God has called us to. Love and anger may not feel like a peanut butter and jelly perfect match, but it just might be the combination that gets you going in your mission!

The People First Called "Christians"

One final thought as we wrap up *Missional U*: Do you know where the name "Christian" originated? You most likely know that it means "little Christ" or "follower of Christ," but where was the name first used?

Acts chapter 11 is where we learn about the people who were first called Christians. It was in a city called Antioch. Antioch is in modern-day Turkey and has been an important city for thousands of years. It's in this city where followers of Jesus first receive the name Christian. Who are these people? Acts 11:20-21 tells us that **"men from Cyprus and Cyrene, went to Antioch and began to speak to Greeks also, telling them the good news about the Lord Jesus. The Lord's hand was with them, and a great number of people believed and turned to the Lord."** Who were these "first Christians" and who first witnessed to them? We don't know. The Scriptures only say that at least some of the first to be called Christians were Greeks (Gentiles) and that men from Cyprus and Cyrene (so most likely also Gentiles) evangelized them.

With all of the great leaders in the early Church: Peter and John (who were part of the original Twelve), Paul (who had a personal and blinding encounter with Jesus on the road to Damascus), James (the brother of Jesus who because the head leader of the Church at Jerusalem), it was not them who first evangelized at Antioch or were first to be called Christians. The first to be called Christians were ordinary people whom God used in extraordinary ways.

I hope you have been wrestling with what a missional life will look like for you. For many of us – dare I say most of us – we can't preach like Paul, we can't pray like Peter, we can't encourage like Barnabus, and we can't love Jesus like John. But all of us can be who God has called us to be. And while we might never be a "celebrity" Christian, neither were the first people called Christians. They just lived a missional life and God used them. May it also be true for us!

The class bell is about to ring, but don't forget that the learning goes on. Learning to be missional is a lifelong process. We shouldn't get discouraged if we struggle and even fail at times. God will continue to provide us with opportunities every day to continue living out that mission trip. You're ready! Class dismissed!

Endnotes

[1] (Page 23) David Ruis. "Every Move I Make." Every Move I Make. Vineyard, 2004.

[2] (Page 147) *Speed*. Dir. Jan de Bont. Twentieth Century Fox, 1994. Film.

[3] (Page 170) *The Lord of the Rings: The Fellowship of the Ring*. Dir. Peter Jackson. New Line Cinema, 2001. Film.

[4] (Page 192) Jon Huckins & Rob Yackley. *Thin Places: Six Postures for Creating & Practicing Missional Community*. (The House Studio: Kansas City, MO, 2013), 33.

[5] (Page 192) Brian M. Howell, *Short-term Missions: An Ethnography of Christian Travel Narrative and Experience*. (Intervarsity Press: Downers Grove, IL, 2012), 221.

[6] (Page 198) *The Avengers*. Dir. Joss Whedon. Walt Disney Studios, 2012. Film.

I'd love to hear how you're doing on your Missional U homework! Drop me a line at jacobyoumans@gmail.com. I know God is going to use you in extraordinary ways to advance His kingdom! Know that I am praying for you and I encourage you to be praying for all of the missionaries – around the world and in your backyard! God's richest blessings!

Mailing Address:
    Dr. Jacob Youmans
    Director, DCE Program
    Assistant Professor of Education
    Concordia-Texas
    11400 Concordia University Drive
    Austin, TX 78726

Also from Tri-Pillar Publishing

MISSIONAL TOO

The Trip of a Lifetime

DR. JACOB YOUMANS

Bon Voyage... Again!

In this second volume of devotions on the joy of missional living, Dr. Jacob Youmans shows us what it means to see the world through redemptive eyes, love the world with an evangelistic heart, and travel the world with the Gospel of peace firmly on our feet. In *Missional Too: The Trip of a Lifetime*, we discover that when we walk in the footsteps of Jesus, the imprint we leave behind is His, not our own – and that makes all the difference. Our journey here as God's dearly loved people is a Gospel-sharing, disciple-making one.

Dr. Jacob Youmans, a dynamic conference speaker, is Director of the DCE Program at Concordia University in Austin, Texas.

$14.95 – Order online at ww.tripillarpublishing.com

Shaking Scripture

Grasping More of God's Word

Rev. Mark Manning

Shaking Scripture was written to help develop a hunger within you for God's Word. You will see how intriguing and interesting the Bible can be. You will be guided through some of the well-known stories we've grown to love and that have, perhaps, gotten stale with familiarity. In addition, you will discover some lesser-known stories that just might surprise you because of their readability and application. In all, there are 12 devotions, each aimed at "Shaking Scripture" in a way that helps us grasp more of God's Word. Several reflective questions per devotion are also provided, making this book ideal for individual or group study.

Rev. Mark Manning serves as Associate Pastor of St. Paul's Lutheran Church in Orange, CA, where he shares his passion for understanding Scripture.

$14.95 – Order online at ww.tripillarpublishing.com

Abba Daddy Do

exploration s in child like faith

by Dr. Jacob Youmans

Join the adventure of childlike faith!

When you're a child, every day is an adventure! Each day you see and experience life for the very first time. Reclaim the wonder and excitement meant for followers of Jesus as we explore the gift of childlike faith. Jacob Youmans, father of two, walks us through 40 true-life stories, discovering the spiritual in the everyday moments of childhood. Complete with study questions and scriptural references, this book is perfect for the individual looking to grow and be challenged, as well as a family or Bible study group.

Dr. Jacob Youmans, a dynamic conference speaker, is Director of the DCE Program at Concordia University in Austin, Texas.

$14.95 – Order online at ww.tripillarpublishing.com

Powerful Love

An Introduction to Christianity

by Rev. Dr. Lloyd Strelow

You've got questions -
God's love provides the answers!

Powerful Love gets to the core of the essence of our Christian faith. The first chapter opens the window to God's love for each of us. It is through that window - guided by the Holy Spirit - that Christians see, believe, and live the rest of God's Word. Throughout Powerful Love, Pastor Strelow uses the inductive method, using our questions to lead us to search God's Word and find His answers for faith and life. Written as a basic guide to the Christian faith, Powerful Love also includes thoughtful study questions and an introductory guide

Rev. Dr. Lloyd Strelow has served six congregations in Michigan and California, including Prince of Peace Lutheran Church (LCMS) in Hemet, CA, where one of his primary emphases was to teach the basics of the Christian faith to all who seek to know the Lord.

$12.95 – Order online at ww.tripillarpublishing.com

tALKING PICTURES

How to turn a trip to the
movies into a mission trip

by Dr. Jacob Youmans
Foreword by Leonard Sweet

Movies and ministry? What's the story?

Movies are everywhere - at the theater, at home, on our computers, even in our pockets! Our culture's fascination with the power of movies brings us together in a shared experience. But did you ever think that watching the latest action-adventure flick with a friend could provide a truly unique opportunity to witness about your Christian faith? Talking Pictures examines the power of movies in our culture and explores effective ways in which we can use any movie as a way to start conversations about our Christian faith.

Dr. Jacob Youmans, a dynamic conference speaker, is Director of the DCE Program at Concordia University in Austin, Texas.

$14.95 – Order online at ww.tripillarpublishing.com

Extraordinary News

for ordinary people

by Rev. Heath Trampe

What's so special about being ordinary?

In a world which equates "ordinary" with "not good enough," Rev. Heath Trampe uses powerful examples from the Bible to prove that even ordinary people can accomplish amazing things. As you journey through these 12 stories of inspiration and hope, you'll discover that "ordinary" is a pretty amazing thing to be. This 214-page book includes Bible study questions for each chapter, with in-depth answers and commentary. It is ideal for both individual and group study.

INDIE 2010 NEXT GENERATION BOOK AWARDS FINALIST!

Reverend Heath Trampe graduated in May 2010 with a Masters of Divinity from Concordia Theological Seminary in Fort Wayne, Indiana. Heath is currently serving as Associate Pastor of St. Peter's Lutheran Church in Fort Wayne.

$14.95 – Order online at ww.tripillarpublishing.com

E-DiBS.org
Daily Bible Studies

You're Invited: Study Your Bible, Grow in Christ!

E-DiBS.org is a free online ministry that delivers a brief, video-based Bible study to your personal e-mail address five days a week.

Led by Pastor Paul Stark, sessions are just 8-10 minutes in length and each video is accompanied by a downloadable PDF file for reading or note-taking.

E-DiBS was designed to help people get into the habit of consistent, daily time in the Word of God by removing the two most common barriers that prevent it: lack of time and lack of understanding. With E-DiBS, all you do is point and click, and you're on your way!

❖ Learn book by book, chapter by chapter, and verse by verse
❖ Share with your friends and family by forwarding the daily e-mail or posting to your Facebook page
❖ Great for individual study time, family devotions, small-group ministry, and workplace sharing
❖ Search and view 1600+ studies at any time via the Bible Study Archive Page

To learn more or sign up, go to www.e-dibs.org, or drop Pastor Stark a line directly at pillar_ministries@yahoo.com.

www.ingramcontent.com/pod-product-compliance
Lightning Source LLC
LaVergne TN
LVHW051510080426
835509LV00017B/2010